THE MIRROR OF

NEW SERIES   VOLUME 49

COSTERUS

Rodopi

AMSTERDAM 1985

THE MIRROR OF EVERYMAN'S SALVATION

A Prose Translation of the
Original *Everyman*

by

ohn Conley, Guido de Baere, H.J.C. Schaap, and W.H. Toppen

* * *

Accompanied by *Elckerlijc* and the
English *Everyman*
Along with Notes

CIP-GEGEVENS

Mirror

The mirror of Everyman's salvation : a prose translation
of the original Everyman / by John Conley . . . [et al.]. —
Amsterdam : Rodopi. — (Costerus. New series ; vol. 49)
Bevat: Elckerlijc en Everyman.
ISBN 90—6203—865—4
SISO Enge 852.7 UDC 820+839.31
Trefw. : Engelse letterkunde / Nederlandse letterkunde.

© Editions Rodopi B.V., Amsterdam
Printed in The Netherlands

Table of Contents

Preface

Since both *Everyman* and the other English translation of *Elckerlijc, The Mirror of Salvation* by Adriaan J. Barnouw,[1] are relatively free, the following relatively close translation, in prose, should be useful to various readers. The need for such a translation has been obscured not only by Middle English scholars in general[2] but also by most recent editors of *Everyman*, who have resorted to hedging on the question of so-called priority,[3] though only a scholar as perverse as Henry de Vocht[4] would deny, after studying the long debate, that *Den Spyeghel der Salicheit van Elckerlijc* — to emphasize its full title[5] — is the original. In his well-known edition of *Everyman* A. C. Cawley provides a handy summary of the debate and remarks, "The only arguments which have not been turned inside out are the ones based on factual evidence, and these point to *Elckerlijc* as the original and to *Everyman* as the translation."[6] Yet Professor Cawley seldom cites *Elckerlijc* and, unduly influenced, apparently, by *Everyman*'s reputation, shrinks from conceding the defects of

1. With the subtitle *A Moral Play of Everyman* c. 1490 (The Hague, 1971).

2. Cf. Donald R. Howard's ambiguous silence on *Elckerlijc* in a recent comment on *Everyman*: "For example, the English morality play *Everyman*, known as a text and specimen, was produced in 1901 by the Elizabethan Stage Society. . . Medieval drama became theater again, and *Everyman* rose above other morality plays as the classic of its genre," "The Four Medievalisms," *University Publishing*, No. 9 (1980), 5.

3. For example, J. B. Trapp, editor of the medieval section of *The Oxford Anthology of English Literature* (New York, 1973), writes, "*Everyman* may be a translation of a Dutch play on the same theme, *Elckerlijc*, but some scholars maintain that the Dutch play is the translation. It is certain that they are closely related" (I, 367). Cf. E. Talbot Donaldson in *The Norton Anthology of English Literature*, rev. ed. (New York, 1970), I, 314.

4. See his *Everyman: A Comparative Study of Texts and Sources* in *Materials for the Study of Old English Drama*, N.S. (Louvain, 1947), 20.

5. The title of *Everyman* has been similarly abbreviated (see the prologue: "The Somonynge of Eueryman called it is" [4]).

6. *Everyman* (Manchester, 1961), p. xi (all quotations from *Everyman* follow this edition). The arguments by E.R. Tigg are especially persuasive; they concern "the evidence of rhymes and formulae" ("Is *Elckerlijc* Prior to *Everyman*?," *Journal of English and Germanic Philology*, 38 [1939], 568). Similarly, J.M. Manly showed that lines 114-18 of *Everyman* reflect a wrong division of the corresponding lines in *Elckerlijc* ("*Elckerlijc-Everyman*: The Question of Priority," *Modern Philology*, 8 [1910], 269-70). Despite Tigg's strictures on "the 'better sense' argument" (*JEGP*, pp. 568-69), it works well *vis à vis Elckerlijc* and *Everyman* if judiciously applied.

this work,[7] while preferring to call the translator "poet" or "author" or at least "author-translator."[8]

Accordingly various errors in the translation are either glossed over or by-passed in this edition. For example, Everyman, in his prayer for forgiveness, fuzzily addresses God as "O goodly vysyon" (582),[9] a phrase never questioned in anthologies of English literature. In this instance Professor Cawley retreats to euphemism: "These words seem to preserve the appearance, though not the meaning, of the Dutch *godlic wesen* 'divine being' (*Elckerlijc* 550)."[10] Earlier, Confession instructs Everyman that he must scourge himself before "thou scape that paynful pylgrymage" (565). Though there is no escaping, Professor Cawley tries to explain the line away: Everyman "has still to make satisfaction. . . before he can hope to finish his pilgrimage and attain eternal bliss."[11] The Dutch refers to another pilgrimage (530-32)[12]: "Peyst dat ons Here oeck was geslaghen/Met geesselen dat Hi woude verdraghen./Recht voer Sijn pelgrimagie stranghe. . ." (Remember that our Lord was beaten/With scourges, which He was willing to endure/Just before His hard pilgrimage. . ."). In Professor Cawley's notes there is nothing on "brytell" (425), where Goods refuses to accompany Everyman: "Nay, not so! I am to brytell; I may not endure." Apparently the translator simply guessed the meaning of "onbranlijc" (394),[13] that is, *adamant*: "Neen, ick bin onbranlijc." Nor is there any com-

7. *Everyman*, especially pp. xxvii-viii in defense of the prosody.

8. Ibid., pp. xxiv-v and xxviii. The translator is referred to as such on p. xiii, however. In a recent edition, much indebted to Cawley's, *Everyman* is presented throughout the first four pages of the introduction as an original play (*The Summoning of Everyman*, ed. Geoffrey Cooper and Christopher Wortham [Nedlands, W. Australia, 1980]; moreover, in the notes I count only ten references to *Elckerlijc*, nearly all in Cawley, and only one, also in Cawley, specifically concerns the adequacy of the translation, the note on lines 575-76.

9. As De Vocht pointed out, in all the other instances of *wesen*, it is correctly translated (*Everyman: A Comparative Study*, p. 36). On the speculation that this error and certain others represent "not what the translator saw but, rather, what he thought that he had heard in dictation," see John Conley, "Aural Error in *Everyman*?," *Notes and Queries*, N. S. (1975), 244-45.

10. *Everyman*, p. 34.

11. Ibid.

12. As G. Kalff pointed out in a review of Henri Logeman's edition of *Elckerlijk. . . and Everyman* in *Taal en Letteren*, 4 (1894), 119. All citations of *Elckerlijc* are to the accompanying text, which, except as cited (see the introduction to the "Notes on the Text of *Elckerlijc*"), follows the lineation of R. Vos's edition, *Den Spieghel der Salicheit van Elckerlijc* (Groningen, 1967). The text of this edition follows the Brussels print except where eked out with the Brussels manuscript.

13. See J. van Mierlo, S. J., *Elckerlijc: Nieuwe Bijdragen met geemendeerde uitgave* (Antwerp, 1949), p. 72; cited below as *Elckerlijc*. On the mistranslation of "ghemeent" (*Elck.* 39), or "loved," as "ment" (*Ev.* 56), see R.W. Zandvoort, "*Everyman-Elckerlijc*," reprinted in *Collected Papers* (Groningen, 1954), pp. 43-44.

ment on Everyman's obtuse second question of Death, in reply to the latter's second question (86), "Hast thou thy Maker forgete?" Everyman: "Why askest thou? / Woldest thou wete? " (87-88).[14]

Though Barnouw's translation is said to be in "modern English,"[15] it is not consistently so, as these lines from God's opening speech indicate (10-17, 23):

> Avarice, hate, envy, pride
> With the seven powerful deadly sins
> Have not [i.e., now] in the world gained prominence.
> For it is because these seven conspire
> That I have opened up my ire,
> Which saddens me and my heavenly host.
> The seven virtues, who once were most,
> Have all been driven away and shent. . .
> All that groweth up worsens on.

As is common in a free translation, there are various embellishments, such as "heaven's radiance" (682) for "the salvation of mankind" ("des menschen salicheyt," 687), and "Grief is carved upon your face" (196) for "One could cut anguish out of you" ("Een mensche mocht druc uut u snijden," 196). Similarly God is interpolated twice within a few lines in one of Death's speeches; thus "be certain about this" ("des seker sijt," 90) is rendered "so God says" (91), and "Also no delay is here befitting" ("Oeck en hoort hier gheen verlaet," 93), "since God has thus decreed" (95). Sometimes the loss in tone and style is considerable: "Loyalty here, loyalty there" (Trou hier, trou daer" 264), or "Such harping on loyalty," becomes "Faith is a perishable fodder" (264). And an especially flat statement in the original appears as an exclamation; thus "I am really glad about that" ("des bin ick rechts ver-huecht," 184) is converted into "O joy!" (184).[16]

Our purpose has been a modest one: to provide as literal a translation of *Elckerlijc* as we could without blurring the meaning or wrenching English usage. Though we have resorted to paraphrase from time to time, most of the translation is word for word, and ordinarily we have not amended where

14. The second question can be regarded as a garbled rendering of Doot's statement in line 71: "Dit suldi wel weten" ("This you will surely know").

15. *Mirror of Salvation*, p. xvi.

16. It is especially regrettable that the names of two of the characters, Duecht (Virtue) and Kennisse (Knowledge), appear as Charity and Contrition respectively. The latter interpretation apparently originated with Francis A. Wood ("*Elckerlijc-Everyman*: The Question of Priority," *Modern Philology*, 8 [1910], 5-7). A grammatical confusion in the translation should also be noted; an antecedent, *Elckerlijc*, has been altered to *Christ*. The original reads (554), "die Adam onterfde bi Yeven rade" ("Whom [i. e., Everyman] Adam disinherited by Eve's advice"). Barnouw's version comes out as "Everyman, who [i. e., Christ] paid / With death for the sin of Adam and Eve" (548-49).

the syntax of the original is awkward or a construction verbose (cf. "ende buten seghe," 68, and "trouwe, die groot is," 261). Emendations are italicized, and interpolations are bracketed. The notes, which were also done in collaboration, are nearly all confined to matters of text and translation; among these are textual cruces and literal renderings of certain passages. Variants are ordinarily supplied only when the text is emended. To help the reader follow the original, the translation appears as if in verse and usually corresponds line for line. Obviously, nothing like an edition proper, with a complete textual apparatus, comprehensive introduction and notes, has been attempted, nor is a bibliography provided; the one in Vos is still relatively up to date for *Elckerlijc*, and there are bibliographies of *Everyman* both in Cawley's edition and Cooper and Wortham's. As for editorial chores, these were performed with the assistance of Dr. de Baere, Drs. Schaap, and Professor Toppen.

The text of *Elckerlijc* provided here is based on the print by Willem Vorsterman (Antwerp, ca. 1518-25). It is the only so-called complete early copy of the work, now in the Leiden University Library; Van Mierlo has argued that *Everyman* derives from this print.[17] The two other prints are earlier: Delft, ca. 1495, and Antwerp, ca. 1501. All three are apparently at least twice removed from the archetype, and all are corrupt. The manuscript of the work, discovered in 1932, though useful, is late (ca. 1593-94).

Certain letters of the Vorsterman print have been modernized according to conventional practice. The line numbering, as already noted, is that of Vos's edition.

To further comparison between the two plays, *Everyman* has been included, according to the Huntington Library copy (ca. 1528-29), which is the earlier of the two complete prints, both by John Skot (or Scott). In keeping with general practice, some of the spelling has been modernized. Various emendations have also been included.

The doctrinal scheme of *Elckerlijc* and *Everyman* is Catholic and emphasizes two articles of faith in particular: the necessity, for salvation, of good works, and divine judgment after death.[18] In time the first of these articles kindled Lutheran revisions of *Elckerlijc*, treated below, as well as latter-day scholarly strictures on *Everyman*.[19]

---

17. *Elckerlijc*, pp. 22 ff. Vos challenged this conclusion in "*Elckerlijc-Everyman-Homulus-Der sünden loin ist der Toid*," *Tijdschrift voor Nederlandse Taal- en Letterkunde*, 82 (1966), 129-43, arguing that *Everyman* derives from an older version of *Elckerlijc* than that of any of the three early prints.

18. Cf. John Conley, "The Doctrine of Friendship in *Everyman*," *Speculum*, 44 (1969), 374.

19. Cf. E. K. Chambers, *English Literature at the Close of the Middle Ages* (Oxford, 1947), p. 64: "I am no theologian, but the strong emphasis on Good Deeds seems to me to suggest a Protestant temper rather than a Catholic one." Some years later Arnold

11

The plot of *Elckerlijc* and *Everyman* consists of a test of friendship made by a worldly young man when he suddenly learns that God has summoned him to his reckoning. The delineation of friendship is in accord with the essential commonplaces of the medieval doctrine of friendship: that no man should be accounted a friend whose friendship has not been tested; that true friendship is lasting; that it is virtuous, indeed supernatural — a gift of God; that, correspondingly, it is precious; finally, that it provides counsel and comfort pertaining not only to this life but also to the next life.[20]

The author of *Elckerlijc* is unknown except as a certain Peter of the Flemish city of Diest (Petrus Diesthemius). Since the late nineteenth century, Petrus Dorlandus (1454-1507), or Peter of Doorlandt, a native of Diest, has been persistently advanced as the probable author.[21] A theologian and Carthusian, he wrote numerous religious works, many of them in dialogue. But no play is mentioned in a long list of his works by a contemporary Carthusian, Andreas of Amsterdam.

In Antwerp, at a rhetorical contest or festival of the sort called a *land-juweel*, *Elckerlijc* was awarded the prize ("palmamque adepta"). Its early history, however, is largely one of various translations, or adaptations, which were often staged. The first such adaptation is a Latin one, *Homulus* (1536), modeled on Plautus and Terence and written by Christianus Ischyrius, or Christiaan de Stercke, rector of the Latin school of Maastricht. Its title page is the source both of the attribution of *Elckerlijc* to Peter of Diest and our knowledge of the prize. Two other Latin adaptations soon followed. The first of these, *Hekastus*, or *Everyman* in Greek, was done by Georgius Macropedius (Joris Langvelt), rector of the Latin school at Utrecht, where the play was first produced a year earlier. In *Hekastus*, by contrast with *Homulus*, which preserves the Catholic character of the original, a Protestant (Lutheran) shading is evident, though the author defended his orthodoxy in the second edition. Nevertheless, Kennisse has been displaced by Fides, and it is she, rather than

Williams quoted this statement as an example of "a certain uneasiness" among "the more perceptive critics" concerning the theology of the two plays, after which he explained Chambers' meaning: "the theology of *Everyman* struck him as different from that with which he was familiar. If he had been a Baptist, he would probably have labelled it Catholic," "The English Moral Play before 1500," *Annuale Mediaevale*, 4 (1963), 20. Williams then commented that, though he is "no theologian" either, he has "read a good bit of theology, and it is my impression that man is saved by grace, not by good deeds. . . There is a theology in which man achieves his salvation through his own efforts, aided by knowledge. This is a fundamental Buddhist tenet, and it ought to come as no surprise [sic] that the original source of *Everyman* is a Buddhist parable" (ibid.).

20. Conley, "Doctrine of Friendship," p. 382. A special version of the traditional classification of goods is implicit in the play — earthly, spiritual, and lasting goods (ibid.).

21. Vos questions this attribution, however, arguing that the language of *Elckerlijc* is scarcely in keeping with a "Carthusian-humanist" and that "the character" of the play is unlike "that of the work of Petrus Dorlandus" (*Den Spieghel der Salicheit*, p. 26).

Virtus, who is Hekastus' chief counsellor and spokesman right to the end. As numerous performances and translations into German, Danish, and Swedish attest, this adaptation was very popular in Protestant circles in the sixteenth and early seventeenth centuries and is the basis of Hans Sachs's *Ein Comedie von dem reichen sterbenden Menschen − A Comedy of the Dying Rich Man* (1549). *Mercator* (*The Merchant*) followed *Hekastus* by one year (1540). It is an out-and-out Protestant adaptation by Thomas Naogeorgus, or Kirchmeyer, with a polemical preface. The dialogue is no less polemical. Along with Mercator three other characters are summoned to judgment before Christ, and all three − Princeps, Episcopus, and Franciscanus − are damned; Mercator, who has been instructed by Paulus and who has learned during his respite to trust in faith, or God, alone, is saved from papist doctrine. The play was translated into French, Polish, Czech, and Russian as well as Dutch and High German. These three adaptations contain numerous characters and are progressively diffuse: *Homulus*, almost twice as long as *Elckerlijc*, runs to 1,539 lines; *Hekastus*, to 1,831, and *Mercator*, to 3,204.[22]

The Low German *Homulus, Der sünden loin ist der Toid* (*Everyman, the Wages of Sin Is Death*) appeared in the same year (1540) as *Mercator* but is a Catholic version, by Jaspar von Gennep, the printer of *Homulus*. It was twice translated into Dutch, once in a Protestant adaptation, which went through six editions by 1700. Another Low German adaptation, a Protestant one by Johannes Stricerius, or Stricker, appeared in 1584 under the title *De Düdesche Schlömer* (*The German Gourmand*). Like Gennep's version, it draws on both *Homulus* and *Hekastus*. As for *Elckerlijc*, it apparently languished meanwhile until the nineteenth century whereas *Everyman* had been reprinted in 1773.

Elckerlijc is itself an adaptation, perhaps the author's own, of the widespread parable of the Faithful Friend, which appears in the oriental tale *Barlaam and Josaphat* and in such famous medieval compilations as the *Gesta Romanorum* and the *Legenda Aurea*. The latter presents the version in *Barlaam and Josaphat*; it runs as follows. In fear of his life after being summoned to appear before the king, a man seeks out his three friends, one of whom he loves more than himself, the second, as much as himself, and the third, for whom he has done little, not at all. The first friend offers him two sackcloths for his burial; the second is willing to accompany him only as far as the gate of the palace; the third, to whom he turns in shame and despair, readily promises to plead for him before the king "lest he hand you over to your enemies." The three friends are then identified in turn as riches; wife, sons, and kindred; faith, hope, alms, and other good works. The king is of course God.

Various debts remain to be acknowledged.

---

22. By comparison the relative fidelity of *Everyman* to *Elckerlijc* is notable.

Vos's edition of *Elckerlijc* should be mentioned first; the editions by A. van Elslander, H. J. E. Endepols, G. Jo Steenbergen, and J. van Mierlo have also been regularly consulted,[23] as well as the diplomatic, parallel-text edition by M.J.M. de Haan and B.J. van Delden.[24]

The translation has benefited from careful and gracious readings by Professor Philip E. Webber of Central College, Iowa, and by Professor Herbert S. Lindenberger of Stanford University. At an early stage Professor C. A. L. Jarrott of Loyola University, Chicago, provided me with her own translation of the first 291 lines of *Elckerlijc*.

For help in a search for requisite scholars of Dutch the following should be mentioned: Professor Stanley M. Wiersma of Calvin College, Michigan, above all; Professor W. M. H. Hummelen of the Catholic University, Nijmegen; Professor Emeritus A.C. Cawley of Leeds University. Nor should I fail to include Professor James J. Wilhelm of Rutgers University, Professor E. G. Stanley of Oxford University, and Mr. Paul J. Meyvaert, editor emeritus of *Speculum*, as well as Professor Derek Pearsall of the University of York and Drs. M. Buning, editor of the *Dutch Quarterly Review*.

The Vorsterman *Elckerlijc* is printed by permission of the Leiden University Library; the earlier of the Skot editions of *Everyman*, by permission of the Huntington Library, San Marino, California. The edition of *Elckerlijc* by Mr. Vos has been used as a basic source for the translation by permission of both the editor and the publishers, Wolters-Noordhoff. In each instance the terms are very generous.

Finally, for typing I am much indebted to Pamela Felmley; for proofreading and much else, to my wife, Eleanor; for counsel, to Mother M. Justin, O.P., formerly of the Dominican College of San Rafael, San Rafael, California, and to Professor Emeritus J.V. Cunningham of Brandeis University, for a copy, many years ago, of one of W.W. Greg's reprints of *Everyman*.

John Conley

23. Van Elslander, *Den Spyeghel der Salicheyt van Elckerlijc* (Amsterdam, 1952); Endepols, *Den Spyeghel der Salicheyt van Elckerlijc* (Groningen, 1925); Steenbergen, *Den Spiegel der Zaligheid van Elckerlijk,* 2nd ed. (Zwolle, 1963); Van Mierlo: see note 13

24. *De Spiegel der Zaligheid van Elkerlijk* (Leiden, 1979), Publication No. 7 of the Vakgroep Nederlandse Taal- en Letterkunde. One should not assume that the transcription is free from error, however. Thus — to cite two examples from the transcription of the Leiden print — *spreeckt* appears as "spreekt" in the incipit (p. 19), and in line 817 (Vos 821) *ghestelt*, as "gheselt."

Addendum

The late E.R. Tigg's privately printed monograph, *The Dutch 'Elckerlijc' Is Prior to the English Everyman* (London, 1981), is reviewed in *Medium Aevum*, 52 (1983), 111-14. (With grateful acknowledgment to Professor Morton W. Bloomfield and Professor Cawley.)

Den Spyeghel der Salicheyt van Elckerlijc

Hoe dat elckerlijc mensche wert
ghedaecht Gode rekeninghe
te doen

Hier beghint een schoon boecxken ghemaeckt in den maniere van eenen speele
ofte esbamente op elckerlijc mensche. Ende inden eersten spreeckt God almachtich aldus:

    Ick sie boven uut mijnen throne
    Dat al dat is int smenschen persone
    Leeft uut vresen, onbekent.
    Oec sie ic tvolc also verblent
5   In sonden, si en kennen mi niet voer God.
    Opten aertschen scat sijn si versot.
    Dien hebben si voer Gode vercoren
    Ende mi vergheten, die hier te voren
    Die doot heb geleden doer tsmenschen profijt.
10 Och, hovaerdie, . . .ghiericheyt ende nijt
    Metten . vij. dootsonden vermoghen,
    Hoe sidi ter werelt nu voert ghetoghen.
    Want mits den .vij. dootsonden gemeen
    Es op ghedaen; des ick in ween
15 Ben seker met alder hemelscher scaren.
    Dye .vij. duechden, dye machtich waren,
    Sijn alle verdreven ende verjaecht;
    Want donnosel heeft mij seer gheclaecht.
    Elckerlijc leeft nu buyten sorghen;
20 Nochtan en weten si ghenen morghen.
    Ick sie wel, hoe ic tvolc meer spare,
    Hoet meer arghert van jare te jare.
    Al dat op wast arghert voert.
    Daer om wil ic nu, als behoert,
25 Rekenninghe van Elckerlijc ontfaen.
    Want liet ic dye werelt dus langhe staen
    In desen leven, in deser tempeesten,
    Tvolc souden werden argher dan beesten
    Ende souden noch deen den anderen eten.
30 Mijn puer ghelove is al vergheten,
    Dat ic hem *selve* gheboot te houden;

How Every Man Is Summoned to Give Reckoning
to God

Here begins a fine book on Everyman made in the manner of a play or play-
let. And at the outset God almighty speaks thus.

    I see above from my throne
    That all that is in the person of man
    Is living without fear, [willfully] ignorant.
    Also I see the people so blinded
5   By sins that they know me not for God.
    Of worldly treasure they are enamored.
    This they worship as God
    And are forgetting me, who heretofore
    Has suffered death for the benefit of man.
10 O pride, avarice, and envy,
    Powerful among the Seven Deadly Sins,
    How you have advanced now throughout the world!
    Because of the Seven Deadly Sins together
    [The door] has been made open; I am therefore surely grieved
15 Along with all the heavenly hosts.
    The Seven Virtues, which were powerful,
    All are driven out and chased away.
    For the innocent have sorely complained of it to me.
    Now every man lives without concern;
20 Yet they do not know any to-morrow.
    I see well how the more I spare the people,
    The worse they get from year to year.
    All that grows up becomes ever worse.
    Therefore I will now, as it is fitting,
25 Receive the reckoning of every man.
    For if I let the world continue thus
    In this life, in this storm,
    The people would become worse than beasts
    And would eat one another up.
30 My pure belief is quite forgotten
    That I *myself* commanded them to keep.

Het *cr*anct, het dwijnt, het staet te couden,
Daer ic so minlijc om sterf die doot,
Ontsculdich, sonder bedwanc oft noot;
35 Om dat ick hoepte dat si bi desen
Mijnder eewigher glorien ghebrukich souden wesen,
Daer icse seer toe hadde vercoren.
Nu vinde ick dattet als is verloren
Dat icse so costelic hadde ghemeent.
40 Hoe menich goet ic hem vry heb verleent
Uut mijnder ontfermherticheydens tresoor,
Dat hem recht toe hoort; nochtans sijnse soe door
Ende verblent int aertsche goet,
Als dat justicie wercken moet
45 Aen Elckerlijc, die leeft so onvervaert.
Waer sidi, mijn Doot, die niemant en spaert?
Coemt hier! hoort wat ic u sal vermonden.
Die Doot.   Tuwen beveele in allen stonden,
Almachtich God, segt U beheet.

God Spreect
50 Gaet hene tot Elckerlijc ghereet
Ende segt hem van mijnen tweghen saen
Dat hi een pelgrimagie moet gaen
Die niemant ter werelt en mach verbi
Ende dat hi rekeninghe come doen mi
55 Sonder vertrec; dats mijn ghebot.
Die Doot.   Het wert ghedaen, almachtich God.
Ick wil ter werelt gaen regneren.
Oeck sal ic rasschelijc, sonder cesseren,
Tot Elckerlijc gaen: hi leeft so beestelic
60 Buten Gods vreese ende alte vreeslick;
Voer God aenbidt hi deertsche goet;
Daer wilic tot hem gaen met snellen keere.
Hi coemt hier gaende; help, God Heere!
Hoe luttel vermoet hi op mijn comen!
65 Ay, Elckerlijc, u wert saen benomen
Dat ghi houden waent seer vast.
Ghi sult staen tot swaren last
Voor Gode almachtich ende buten seghe.
Elckerlijc, waer sidi op weghe
70 Dus moey? hebdi al Gods vergheten?
Elckerlijc.   Waerbi vraechdijs?

It weakens, it languishes, it becomes cold,
For which I so lovingly died the death,
Innocent, without constraint or necessity,
35 Because I hoped that by means of this
They would enjoy my everlasting glory,
For which I had dearly chosen them.
Now I find that it is entirely tor naught
That I loved them at such a price.
40 How many goods I have freely lent them
Out of the treasure of my mercy,
So that they belong to them by right; nevertheless, they are so foolish
And blinded by earthly goods
That justice must be done
45 On Everyman, who is living so fearlessly.
Where are you, my Death, who spares no one?
Come here. Listen to what I shall say to you.
Death. At your command at any time,
Almighty God, speak your command.

50 *God speaks.* Go hence to Everyman at once
And tell him in my name, immediately,
That he must go [on] a pilgrimage
Which no one in the world can avoid
And that he shall come to make his reckoning to me
55 Without delay; that's my command.
Death. It shall be done, almighty God.
I shall go to reign in the world.
Also I shall quickly, without delay,
Go to Everyman; he lives so bestially,
60 Without fear of God and very callously;
He worships earthly goods as God;
Now I shall go to him quickly.
Here he comes walking; help, Lord God,
How little he expects my coming!
65 Oh, Everyman, you will soon be deprived of
What you think you hold very firmly.
You shall stand under a heavy accusation
And defeated before God almighty.
Everyman, where are you going
70 Thus dressed up? Have you forgotten God completely?
Everyman. Why do you ask this?

Die Doot.   Dit suldi wel weten
Wilt na mi hooren te desen stonden.
Naerstich bin ic aen u ghesonden
Van Gode uut des Hemels pleyn.
75 *Elckerlijc.*   Aen mij ghesonden?
Die Doot.   Jae ick, certeyn!
Al hebdi Sijns vergheten, alst blijct,
Hi peynst wel om u in Sijn rijck,
Alsoe ick u sal voer oghen legghen.
Elckerlijc.   Wat begheert God van my?
Die Doot.   Dat sal ick di segghen:
80 Rekenninghe wilt Hi van u ontfaen
Sonder eenich verdrach.
Elckerlijc.   Hoe sal ic dat verstaen?
Rekeninghe? wat salt bedien?
Die Doot.   Al ghevet u vreemt, het moet ghescieden.
Oec moetti aen nemen sonder verdrach
85 Een pelgrimagie, die niemant en mach
Weder keeren in gheender manieren.
Brengt u ghescriften ende u pampieren
Met u ende oversietse bedachtich;
Want ghi moet voer God almachtich
90 Rekenninghe doen, des seker sijt,
Ende hoe ghi bestaet hebt uwen tijt,
Van uwen wercken, goet ende quaet.
Oeck en hoort hier gheen verlaet
Van dien; als nu het moet wesen,
95 Ende oec het moet nu gheschien.
Elckerlijc.   Daer op ben ic nu al qualic versien,
Rekeninghe te doen voer Gode bloot.
Wie bistu bode?
Die Doot.   Ick ben die doot, die niemant en spaert;
100 Maer Elckerlijck sal bi
Gods beveele doen rekeninghe mi.
Elckerlijc.   Och, Doot, sidi mi soe bi,
Als icker alder minst op moede.
Doot, wildi van *mi* hebben goede?
105 Duysent pont sal ic u gheven
Op dat ic behouden mach mijn leven
Ende doet *mi een* verdrach van desen.
Die Doot.   Elckerlijc, dat en mach niet wesen.
Ick en aensie goet, schat noch have;
110 Paeus, hertoghe, coninc, noch grave

Death.　　　　　This you will surely know;
Listen to me in this hour:
Urgently I have been sent to you
By God from the plain of Heaven.
75 *Everyman.* Sent to me?
Death.　　　　　Yes, certainly.
Although you have forgotten Him, as it appears,
He does indeed think of you in His kingdom,
As I shall make clear to you.
Everyman. What does God want of me?
Death.　　　　　That I shall tell you:
80 A reckoning He wants to receive from you
Without any delay.
Everyman. How am I to take that?
Reckoning? What does it mean?
Death. Although it seems strange to you, it has to be.
Also you must undertake without delay
85 A pilgrimage from which no one can
Return by any means.
Bring your writings and your papers
With you and look them over carefully,
For you must, before God almighty,
90 Make a reckoning — be certain about this —
And of how you have spent your time,
Of your works, good and evil.
Also no delay is here befitting
Regarding this. Now it must be,
95 And now it must also come to pass.
Everyman. Just now I am scarcely prepared for that,
Plainly to give a reckoning before God.
Who are you, messenger?
Death.　　　　　I am Death, who spares no one.
100 But every man shall, by
God's command, give a reckoning to me.
Everyman. Oh, Death, are you so near to me
When I am least prepared for it!
Death, do you want money from me?
105 A thousand pounds will I give you
That I may keep my life,
And grant *me a* respite in this regard.
Death. Everyman, that cannot be.
I pay no attention to goods, treasure, or chattels;
110 Pope, duke, king, or count

En spare ic niet nae Gods *ghebieden*.
Waer ic met schatte te verleeden,
Ick creghe wel alder werelt goet.
Nu houtet al met mi den voet.
115 Oec en gheve ic uutstel noch verdrach.
Elckerlijc.   Allendich, arm katijf, o wach!
Nu en weet ick mijns selfs ghenen raet
Van rekenninghe te doen: mijn pampier
Es so verwerret ende so beslet,
120 Ic en sier gheen mouwen toe gheset;
So is mijn herte om desen in vaer.
Och mocht ic noch leven ·xij. jaer,
So soudic mijn ghescrifte exponeren
Ende oversien; wilt doch cesseren
125 Als nu, lieve Doot, van wraken,
Tot dat ic versien bin op die saken.
Dat *bid* ic *u* doer Gods ontfermen.
Die Doot.   U en mach baten smeken oft kermen.
Dus siet wat u staet te beghinnen.
130 *Elckerlijc.*   Lieve Doot, een sake doet mi bekennen:
Al yst dat ic dese vaert moet aengaen,
Soudic niet moghen wederkeeren saen,
Als ic mijn rekeninghe hadde ghestelt?
Die Doot.   Neen ghi, nemmermeer!
Elckerlijc.   Almoghende Gods ghewelt!
135 Wilt mijns ontfermen in deser noot!
En soudic niemant, cleyn noch groot,
Daer moghen leyden, had ict te doene?
Die Doot.   Jae ghi, waer yemant so koene
Dat hi die vaert met u bestonde.
140 Spoet u, want God, die alle gronde
Doersiet met Sinen godliken oghen,
Begheert dat ghi voer Hem coemt toghen
U rekenninghe van dat ghi hebt bedreven.
Wat meendi, dat u hier is ghegheven
145 Tleven op daerde ende tijtlijc goet?
Elckerlijc.   Ay lazen, dat waendick!
Die Doot.   Hoe sidi aldus onvroet,
Elckerlijc, daer ghi hebt vijf sinnen,
Dat ghi soe onsuver sijt van *b*innen
Ende ic so haestelijc come onversien.
150 *Elckerlijc.*   Allendich katijf! waer sal ic vlien,
Dat ic af quame deser groter sorghen?

I spare not in keeping with God's *command*.
If I could be tempted with treasure,
I should certainly get all the world's goods.
Now everyone goes with me on foot.
115 Consequently I give neither delay nor respite.
Everyman. Miserable, poor wretch, O woe!
Now I do not know what to do with myself
About the reckoning: my paper
Is so muddled and so encumbered,
120 I see no way out.
Therefore my heart is afraid because of this.
Oh, if I might live for another twelve years,
Then I would put my records in order
And review them; now please stop [speaking],
125 Dear Death, of punishment
Until I am prepared for this business.
That I beseech you by God's mercy.
Death. Neither entreating nor groaning can do you any good!
Therefore think what you should do.
130 *Everyman.* Dear Death, let me know one thing:
Though . . . I must undertake this journey,
Could I not return soon
When I would have settled my reckoning?
Death. No, never!
Everyman.   Almighty power of God!
135 Have pity on me in this need!
Could I take no one, low or high,
Along there if I should want it?
Death. Yes, if there were anyone so bold
That he would dare to undertake that journey with you.
140 Make haste, for God, who penetrates all depths
With His divine eyes,
Wants you to come before Him to show
Your reckoning of what you have done.
What do you think, that you were here given
145 Life on earth and worldly goods?
Everyman. Alas, so I thought!
Death.   How can you be so foolish,
Everyman, since you have five senses,
That you are so impure *within*
And [that] I so quickly come unexpectedly?
150 *Everyman.* Miserable wretch, where shall I flee
That I might get rid of this great worry?

Lieve Doot, verdraghet mi tot morghen,
Dat ic mi bespreken mach van desen.
Die Doot.   Dat en wil ic niet consenteren in desen,
155   Noch en doe icx niet in gheender tijt;
Ick slae den sulcken ter stont int crijt
Sonder voer raet, met eenen slach.
Aldus bereyt u in desen dach.
Ick wil uut uwen oghen vertrecken.
160   Siet dat ghi u naerstelic gaet betrecken
Te segghen: nu coemt den dach
Die Elckerlijc niet voer bi en mach.
Elckerlijc.   Ay, Elckerlijc, wat dede ic ye gheboren!
Ick sie mijn leven al verloren,
165   Nu ic doen moet dese langhe vaert,
Daer ic so qualic teghen ben bewaert.
Ic en hebbe noyt goet bedreven,
Aldus heb ic seer luttel ghescreven.
Hoe sal ic mi excuseren int claer?
170   Ey lacen, ic woude dat ic nu niet en waer!
Dat waer mijnder sielen groot toeverlaet.
Waer mach ic nu soecken troost of raet?
God die Heere, die alle dinc voersiet,
Dat ic veel claghe, ten helpt niet.
175   Den tijt gaet verre, tes nae noene.
Ay lasen, wat staet mi nu te doene!
Wien mocht ic claghen dese sake?
Laet sien, oft ic mijn Gheselscap sprake
Ende leyde hem te voren om mede te trecken.
180   Soudt hijt mi ontseggen? neen hi, ick wane.
Wi hebben ter werelt in onsen daghen
So groten vrientscap tsamen gedraghen;
Want ic betro*u* hem alder duecht.
Ick sien, des bin ic rechts verhuecht.
185   Oec wil ic hem toe spreken sonder verdrach.
Goeden dach, Gheselscap!
Gheselscap.   Elckerlijc, goeden dach
Moet u God gheven ende ghesonde!
Hoe siedi dus deerlic? doet mi orconde:
Hebdi yet sonderlings dat u let?
190   *Elckerlijc.*   Jae ick, Gheselscap.
·*Gheselscap.*   Achermen, hoe sidi dus ontset!
Lieve Elckerlijc, ontdect mi *uwen noot.*
Ic blive u bi tot in die doot,

Dear Death, give me respite till to-morrow
So that I can deliberate concerning this.
Death. That I will not consent to in this case,
155   Nor will I ever do so at any time.
I smite many a one in the lists at once,
Unexpectedly, at one stroke.   *with dart*
Therefore prepare yourself on this day.
I shall withdraw from your eyes.
160   See that you seriously begin
To say: now comes the day
That Everyman cannot avoid.
Everyman. Oh, Everyman, why was I ever born?
I see my life entirely wasted
165   Now that I must make this long journey
For which I am so badly prepared.
I have never done any good in the world;
Thus I have written very little.
How shall I justify myself clearly?
170   Alas, would that I did not exist now!
That would be a great comfort to my soul.
Where could I now seek help or counsel?
Lord God, who foresees all things,
It does not help that I greatly lament.
175   Time is getting on; 'tis past noon.
Alas, what am I to do now?
To whom could I lament over this matter?
Let [me] see, if I should speak to Fellowship
And suggest that he go with me,
180   Would he refuse it? No, I think —
In the world in our days we have had
Such great friendship together —
For I expect only good from him.
I see him; I am really glad about that.
185   Therefore I will speak to him without delay.
Good day, Fellowship!
Fellowship.   Everyman, a good day
May God give you, and health!
Why are you so sad? Tell me,
Do you have something unusual that troubles you?
190   *Everyman.* Yes, Fellowship.
Fellowship.   Poor fellow, why are you so upset?
Dear Everyman, show me *your need.*
I shall stay with you until death,

Op goet gheselscap ende trou ghesworen!
Elckerlijc.   Ghi segt wel, Gheselscap. Want tes verloren!
195 *Gheselscap.*   Ick moet al weten, u druc, u lijden.
Een mensche mocht druc uut u snijden!
Waer u mesdaen, ic helpt u wreken,
Al soudicker bliven doot ghesteken
Ende ick wiste te voren *claer*.
200 *Elckerlijc.*   Danc hebt, Gheselscap.
Gheselscap.   Ghenen danck een haer!
Daer by segt mi u doghen.
Elckerlijc.   Gheselle, oft ick u leyde voer oghen
Ende u dien last viel te swaer,
Dan soude ic mi meer bedroeven daer.
205 Maer ghi segt wel, God moets u lonen.
Gheselscap.   Way, ic meyne*t*, al sonder honen.
Elckerlijc.   Ghi segt wel, boven screve;
Ic en vant noyt anders aen u dan trouwe.
Gheselscap.   So en suldi oeck nemmermeer!
Elckerlijc.   God loons u ende ons Vrouwe!
210 Gheselle, ghi hebt mi wat verhuecht!
Gheselscap.   Elckerlijc, en sijt niet versaecht.
Ick gae met u, al waert in die Helle.
Elckerlijc.   Ghi spreect als een *goet* gheselle.
Ic sal u danck en als ic best kan.
215 *Gheselscap.*   Daer en is gheen dancken aen.
Diet niet en dade in wercken aenschijn.
Hi en waer niet waert gheselle te sijn.
Daer om wilt mi uwen last ontdecken
Als ghetrouwe vrient.
Elckerlijc.   Ick salt u vertrecken
220 Hier nu seker, al sonder veysen.
Mi es bevolen dat ic moet reysen
Een grote vaert, hardt ende stranghe.
Oec moet ic rekeninge doen bi bedwange
Voer den hoochsten Coninc almachtich.
225 Nu bid ic u, dat ghi zijt bedachtich
Mede te gaen, so ghi hebt beloeft.
Gheselscap.   Dats wel blikelijc;
Die ghelofte houdic van waerden.
Mer soudic sulcken reyse aenvaerden
230 Om beden wille, mi souts verdrieten;
Ic soude van desen gheruchte verscieten.
Mer doch willen wi dbeste doen

Sworn on good fellowship and faith.

Everyman. Well said, Fellowship, for it is lost!

195 *Fellowship.* I must know wholly your anguish, your suffering.
One could cut anguish out of you!
If any harm were done to you, I shall help you to avenge it
Even though I should be stabbed to death
And I knew it *clearly* beforehand.

200 *Everyman.* Thank you, Fellowship!
Fellowship.   No thanks at all!
Therefore tell me your grief.
Everyman. Fellow, if I should make [it] clear
And the burden should be too heavy for you,
Then I would be more distressed.

205 But you [do] speak well; may God reward you for it.
Fellowship. Well, I mean *it* wholly, without deceit.
Everyman. You speak well, immeasurably.
I have never found anything but loyalty in you.
Fellowship. And you always will!
Everyman.   May God and our Lady reward you for it.

210 Fellow, you have somewhat strengthened me.
Fellowship. Everyman, do not be faint-hearted.
I will go with you even though it were to Hell.
Everyman. You speak like a *good* fellow;
I shall reward you as best I can.

215 *Fellowship.* There is no [need of] thanks.
He who would not prove it in deeds
Were not worthy to be a fellow.
Therefore show me your trouble
As a true friend.
Everyman.   I shall tell it to you

220 Here now certainly, entirely without dissembling.
I have been ordered that I must go on
A long journey, hard and severe.
Also I must give a reckoning by command
Before the highest King almighty.

225 Now I pray you that you be minded
To go with me as you have promised.
Fellowship. That's quite obvious;
The promise I consider binding.
But should I undertake such a journey

230 [Only] because of a request, I would regret it.
I should be frightened of this misery,
But still we will do the best [we can]

Ende ons beraden.
Elckerlijc.   Och, hoort doch dit sermoen!
Seydi mi niet, had icx noot,
235 Mede te gaen tot inder hellen doot
Oft in die Helle, had ict begaert?
Gheselscap.   Dat soudic seker, maer sulc ghevaert
Es uut ghesteken, plats metten ronsten!
Om waer seggen, oft wi die vaert begonsten,
240 Wanneer souden wij weder comen na desen?
Elckerlijc.   Daer en is gheen weder keeren.
Gheselscap.   So en wil icker niet wesen.
Wie heeft u die bootscap ghebracht?
Elckerlijc.   Ay lazen, die Doot!
Gheselscap.   Help, heylighe Gods *cracht*!
Heeft die Doot gheweest die bode?
245 Om al dat leven mach van Gode
En ghinc icker niet, mocht icx voerbi.
Elckerlijc.   Ghi seydet mi nochtans toe.
Gheselscap.   Dat kenne ick vry.
Waert te drincken een goet ghelaghe,
Ick ghinc met u totten daghe,
250 Oft waert ter kermissen buten der stede,
Oft daer die schone vrouwen waren.
Elckerlijc.   Daer ghingdi wel mede.
Waert altoos met ghenuechten te gaen, soe waerdi bereet.
Gheselscap.   Hier en wil ic niet mede, God weet,
Maer woudi pelgrimagie gaen,
255 Oft woudi yemant doot slaen,
Ic hulpen ontslippen tot in die broock
Ende oec cloven ontween.
Elckerlijc.   Och, dat is een sober bescheen!
Gheselle, ghi wilt *al* anders dan ick
260 Alst noot is.
Gheselle, peyst om trouwe, die groot is,
Die wi deen den anderen beloeft hebben
Over menich jaer.
Gheselscap.   Trou hier, trou daer!
265 Ic en wilder niet aen, daer mede gesloten.
Elckerlijc.   Noch bid ic, en hadt u niet verdroten,
Doet mi uut gheleye, maect mi moet,
Tot voer die poerte.
Gheselscap.   Tjacob! ic en sal niet eenen voet!

And deliberate.
Everyman.   Oh, listen indeed to this sermonizing!
Didn't you promise me, if I had need of it,
235 To go with me into infernal death
Or into Hell had I the desire for it?
Fellowship. That I certainly would, but such a journey
Is out of the question, to put it bluntly.
To speak the truth, if we set out on the journey,
240 When should we come back after this?
Everyman. There is no coming back.
Fellowship.   Then I don't want to be there.
Who has brought you the message?
Everyman. Alas, Death!
Fellowship.   Help, holy power of God!
Has Death been the messenger?
245 For anything that God allows to live
I should not go if I could avoid it.
Everyman. You promised it, nevertheless.
Fellowship.   That I admit frankly.
If it were for a stiff drinking-bout,
I would go with you until daybreak,
250 Or if it were to go to the fair, outside the city,
Or to where the pretty women would be.
Everyman.   You would certainly [go] with [me] there.
If it were only to go out for pleasure, then you were willing.
Fellowship. Here I will not [go] with [you], God knows,
But if you wanted to go [on] a pilgrimage
255 Or if you wanted to kill somebody,
I would help strip him to the breech
And cleave in two.
Everyman. Oh, that is a poor response!
Fellow, you want it entirely different from me
260 Now that need arises.
Fellow, think on the loyalty, which is great,
That we promised one another
Many years ago.
Fellowship. Such harping on loyalty!
265 I do not wish it; that's that.
Everyman. Nevertheless, I beseech [you], if it were not unwelcome to
[you,

Show me out, give me courage,
Up to the gates.
Fellowship.   By Jacob, I shall not one step!

270 Mer haddi ter werelt noch ghebleven,
Ick en hadde u nemmermeer begheven.
Nu moet u ons lieve Here gheleyden.
Ick wil van u scheyden.
Elckerlijc.   Es dat ghescheyden
Sonder omsien? ay lazen, jaet!
275 Nu sien ic wel, tes cranck toeverlaet,
Tgheselscap, alst coemt ter noot.
Mer waer ic noch in weelden groot
So soudtmen met mi lachen alteenen.
Mer lazen! men wilt met mi niet weenen.
280 Men siet: in voerspoet vintmen vrient
Die ter noot niet zeer en dient.
Een ander hem castie bi desen.
Waer wil ic nu troost soeckende wesen?
Ic weet wel: aen mijn Vrient ende Maghe.
285 Dien wil ic minen noot gaen claghen.
Al is mi mijn Gheselscap af ghegaen,
Si moeten mi doch ter noot bi staen.
Want men doet int ghemeen ghewach
Dattet bloet cruypet daert *niet* wel gaen en mach.
290 Ic salt besoecken op dat ic leve.
Waer sidi, Vrienden ende Maghe?
Maghe.   Hier zijn wi, Neve,
Tuwen ghebode, stout ende koene.
Neve.   Elckerlijc, hebdi ons te doene?
Dat segt ons vry.
Maghe.   Ja, sonder verlaet.
295 Wi zijn tuwen besten, wat ghi bestaet.
Al woudi yemant doot slaen,
Wi helpen u daer toe.
Neve.   Want het moet alsoe staen,
Salment maechscap te recht orboren.
Elckerlijc.   God die danc u, mijn vrienden vercoren.
300 Ick claghe u met droevigher herten mijn ghevaernis,
Dat ic ontboden bin, alsoot claer is,
Een verre pelgrimagie te gaen,
Daer nemmermeer en is wederkeeren aen.
Daer moet ic rekeninge doen, die swaer is,
305 Voerden Heere, diet al openbaer is.
Maghe.   Waer af moetti rekeninghe doen?
Elckerlijc.   Van mijnen wercken, om cort sermoen,

270 But had you still remained in the world,
   I should never have forsaken you.
   Now may our dear Lord accompany you.
   I will part from you.
   Everyman.   Is that parting
   Without looking back? Alas, indeed!
275 Now I see well it's a weak support,
   Fellowship, when need arises.
   But were I still in great prosperity,
   People would laugh with me all the time.
   But, alas, they will not weep with me.
280 It is said, in prosperity one finds [a] friend
   Who is of little use in need.
   Let this be a warning to others.
   Where shall I be looking for help now?
   I know well: with my friends and kinsmen;
285 To them I will go to complain of my distress.
   Although my Fellowship has deserted me,
   They will surely stand by me in distress.
   For it is a common saying
   That blood creeps where it may not go well.
290 I shall test it that I may live.
   Where are you, friends and kinsmen?
   Kinsman.   Here we are, nephew,
   At your command, bold and brave.
   Nephew. Everyman, have you need of us?
   Tell us so frankly.
   Kinsman.   Yes, without delay.
295 We are [here] for your benefit, whatever you may undertake.
   Even if you wanted to kill somebody,
   We would help you with that.
   Nephew.   For so it must be
   If one will rightly practice kinship.
   Everyman. May God reward you, my dear friends.
300 I complain to you, with a sad heart, of my plight,
   That I have been ordered, as it is clear,
   To go [on] a far pilgrimage
   From which there is nevermore a returning.
   There I must give a reckoning that is hard
305 Before the Lord, to whom it all is manifest.
   Kinsman. Of what must you give reckoning?
   Everyman. Of my works, to be brief;

Hoe ic hier mijnen tijt heb versleten
Op aertrijc ende met sonden verbeten,
310 Ende wat ic heb bedreven
Den tijt, gheleent ende niet ghegheven.
Hier wilt doch mede gaen, dat u die almachtige God wil lonen,

Ende helpt mijn rekeninghe verschoonen;
So sal te minder werden mijn seer.
315 *Maghe.*　　　Wat! daer mede te gaen?
Neve.　　　　　　Way, schillet niet meer?
Voerwaer, ick heb een ander ghepeyst.
Maghe.　　Ic valle op mijn achterhielen!
Neve.　　　　　Ten docht niet gheveyst.
Ic seynder mijnre maerten bli ende vry;
Si gaet gaerne ter feesten!
320 *Maghe.*　　　　Ick segghe oeck alsoe.
Ick soude verschieten int laetste.
Elckerlijc.　　En wildi dan niet mede gaen?
Neve.　　　　En laet niet haesten, beste.
Ten is tot gheenre feesten te gaen,
325 Noch tot gheenre sollen!
Elckerlijc.　　　Nu, om een eynde te knopen,
Segt, wildi mede, sonder verlaet?
Maghe.　　Neve, ic neme uutstel, dach ende raet,
Ende mijn ghenachte tot open tijde.
Neve.　　Wi willen ons verblasen.
330 *Elckerlijc.*　　　Hoe soude ick verbliden:
Wat schoonder woerden men mi biet,
Alst coemt ter noot, so eest al niet.
Ay lazen! hoe ist hier ghevaren!
Neve.　　Elckerlijc, neve, God moet u bewaren.
335 Ic en wil niet mede, opt platte gheseyt.
Oec heb ic uutstaende te rekenen wat,
Daer ben ic noch qualic op versien.
Dus blive ic hier.
Elckerlijc.　　　　Dat mach wel zijn.
Tfy, Elckerlijc, hebdi u verlaten
340 Op u mage? die hem so vroemlijc vermaten,
Laten u bliven in desen doghen.
Siet, oftmense jaechde van hier.
Ick sie: men spreect wel metten monde,
Buyten der daet, uut geveynsden gronde.
345 Dan seghen si: neve, ghebreect u yet

How I have dissipated my time here
On earth and wasted in sins,
310 And of what I have done
During the time, lent and not given.
Please go with me on this [journey], that the almighty God may reward
[you,

And help to clear my reckoning;
Then the less will be my grief.
315 *Kinsman.* What! Go with you there!
Nephew. Well, is not something more the matter?
Truly, I have another idea.
Kinsman. I am knocked over!
Nephew. It would be no use to feign.
I will send there my maid gladly and cheerfully;
She likes to go to feasts.
320 *Kinsman.* So I say, too.
I would be frightened at the last.
Everyman. Will you then not go with me?
Nephew. Don't hurry so fast.
It is not [a question of] going to any feast
325 Nor to any game.
Everyman. Now, to make an end of it,
Say, will you [go] with [me], without delay?
Kinsman. Nephew, I shall take a delay, time, and counsel,
And my fortnight until the proper time.
Nephew. We wish a breathing spell.
330 *Everyman.* How could I be glad!
Whatever fine words they offer to me,
When the need comes, then it is all nothing.
Alas, how it has turned out here!
Nephew. Everyman, nephew, may God keep you!
335 I will not [come] with [you], bluntly speaking.
I also have a reckoning to settle
For which I am still badly prepared.
So I shall stay here.
Everyman. Be that as it may.
Fie, Everyman, did you put trust
340 In your kinsman? They who promised so bravely
Let you remain in this suffering.
See, [they flee] as if one drove them from here.
I see: one speaks well with one's mouth,
Without the deed, out of hypocrisy.
345 Then they say, "Nephew, if you lack anything,

Ic ben tuwen besten; tes seker nyet.
Ende des ghelijc seyt tGheselscap, doch
Tes al zoringhe ende bedroch.
Die wil, macher hem toe verlaten.
350   Waer mocht ic mi nu henen saten?
Hier is verloren langhe ghebleven.
Wat vrienden sullen mi nu troost geven?
Daer coemt mi wat nieus inne:
Ic heb aen mijn goet geleyt grote minne.
355   Wilde mij dat helpen tot mijnen orboren,
So en had ict noch niet al verloren.
Ic heb op hem noch alle mijn troost.
O Heere, diet al sal doemen,
Wilt u gracie op mi ontsluyten!
360   Waer sidi, mijn Goet?
Tgoet.   Ick legghe hier in muten,
Versockelt, vermost, als ghi mi siet.
Vertast, vervuylt; ic en kan mi niet
Verporren, also ic ben tsamen gesmoert.
Wat wildi mi hebben?
Elckerlijc.   Coemt rasch hier voert,
365   Lichtelic, Goet, ende laet u sien.
Ghi moet mi beraden.
Tgoet.   Wat rade sal u van mi gheschien?
Hebdi ter werelt eenich letten,
Dat sal ic u beteren.
Elckerlijc.   Tes al een ander smette.
Ten is niet ter werelt, wilt mi verstaen.
370   Ick bin ontboden daer ic moet gaen
Een grote pelgrimagie sonder verdrach.
Oec moet ic, dat is mij tswaerste gelach,
Rekeninghe doen voerden oversten Heere,
Om dwelc ic troost aen u begheere.
375   Mitsdien dat ic in kintschen tijden
Hadde in u groot verblijden
Ende dat mijnen troest al aen u stoet,
So bid ic u, mijn uutvercoren Goet,
Dat ghi met mi gaet sonder cesseren;
380   Want ghi mocht mi licht voer Gode pureren,
Want tGoet kan suveren smetten claer.
Tgoet.   Neen, Elckerlijc, ic mocht u letten daer.
Ic en volghe niemant tot sulcker reisen.
Ende al ghinghe ic mede, wilt peisen,

I am [here] for your benefit; it's certainly nothing,"
And Fellowship speaks in the same manner; yet
It's all deception and imposture.
Who wishes may rely on it.
350 Where could I turn to now?
To remain here longer is useless.
Which friends would give me help now?
Something new comes to me:
To my goods I have given great love.
355 If that would help me to my benefit,
I should not yet have lost it all.
From him I still expect all my help.
O Lord, Who shall judge all,
Open to me Thy grace.
360 Where are you, my Goods?
Goods.   I lie here in a cage,
Neglected, rusty, as you see me,
Heaped up, filthy; I cannot
Stir, pressed as I am together.
What do you want of me?
Everyman.   Come forward here quickly,
365 Promptly, Goods, and let yourself be seen.
You must counsel me.
Goods. What counsel must you have of me?
If something in the world [is] troubling [you],
That I shall put right for you.
Everyman. It is an entirely different trouble.
It is not in the world, do understand.
370 I have been summoned to where I must go [on]
A long **pilgrimage** without delay.
Also I must give — that is the hardest score for me —
A reckoning before the Lord most high,
Wherefore I seek help from you.
375 Because, in my youth,
I had in you great joy
And all my help has rested in you,
Therefore I beg you, my beloved Goods,
That you go with me without delay;
380 For you could easily clear me before God,
For goods can wipe out stains completely.
Goods. No, Everyman, I might hinder you there.
I follow no man on such a **journey**.
And if I went along with you, consider,

385 So soudi mijns te wors hebben grotelic;
Bi redenen, ic salt u segghen blotelijc:
Ic heb zeer u pampier verweert;
Want al u sinnen hebdi verteert
Aen mi; dat mach u leet zijn.
390 Want u rekeninghe sal onghereet zijn
Voer God almachtich, mits minen scouwen.
Elckerlijc. Dat mach mi wel berouwen,
Als ict verantwoerden sal moeten strangelic.
Op, ga wi mede!
Tgoet. Neen, ick bin onbranlijc.
395 Aldus en volghe ic u niet een twint.
Elckerlijc. Ay lazen! ick heb u oeck ghemint
Mijn leefdaghe tot opten tijt van nu.
Tgoet. Dat es een eewige verdomenis voer u:
Mijn minne es contrarye des Hemels staten.
400 Maer haddi mi *ghemint* bi maten
Ende van mi ghedeylt den armen,
So en dorfstu nu niet kermen,
Noch staen bedroeft dat u nu swaer is.
Elckerlijc. Ay lazen, God, ic ken dat waer is.
405 *Tgoet.* Waendi dat ic u bin?
Elckerlijc. Ick hadt ghemeent.
Tgoet. Swijcht, ic en bin mer u gheleent
Van Gode; *Hy proeft*, claer alst is voer oghen,
Hoe ghi sult in weelden poghen.
Die menighe blijft bi mi verloren
410 Meer dan behouden, weet dat te voren.
Waendi dat ic u sal volghen, Elckerlijc,
Van deser werelt? neen ic, sekerlijc!
Elckerlijc. Dat waende ic claerlijc,
Om dat ic u oyt hadde so lief.
415 *Tgoet.* Daer om tGoet kenne ic der sielen dief.
Als ghi nu van hier zijt, dat en mach niet lieghen,
Soe wil ic eenen anderen bedrieghen,
Ghelijc ic dede voer uwen tijt.
Elckerlijc. Och, valsche Goet, vermaledijt!
420 Hoe hebdi mi in u net bevaen,
Verrader Gods.
Tgoet. Ghi hebt dat al u selven ghedaen;
Dat mi lief es te deser tijt.
Ic moet daer om lachen.
Elckerlijc. Sidi dies verblijt,

385 You would be far worse off on account of me.
With reason I will say it to you bluntly:
I have disarranged your account very much,
For your whole being you have wasted
On me; you may be sorry for that,
390 For your reckoning will not be in order
Before God almighty through my fault.
Everyman. I may well repent that
When I shall have to give of it a strict account.
Up! Let us go together!
Goods. No, I am adamant.
395 Therefore I will not follow you at all.
Everyman. Alas, I on the contrary loved you
My whole life till the present moment.
Goods. That means for you an everlasting damnation:
Love of me is contrary to the heavenly state,
400 But had you *loved* me in moderation
And dealt out from me to the poor,
Then you would not need to moan now
Nor be sad, which is grievous to you now.
Everyman. Alas, God, I admit that is true.
405 *Goods.* Do you think that I am yours?
Everyman. I had thought so.
Goods. Silence! I have been only lent to you
By God; *He tests*, clear as it is before [one's] eyes,
How you shall conduct [yourself] in wealth.
Many more are lost through me
410 Than saved, know that for sure.
Did you think that I would follow you, Everyman,
Out of the world? No, certainly [not].
Everyman. That I certainly thought
Because I always loved you so.
415 Therefore I know Goods [to be] the thief of souls.
When you are [gone] from here now, that cannot fail —
So I will deceive another
Just as I did before your time.
Everyman. O false Goods, cursed,
420 How you have caught me in your net,
Traitor to God!
Goods. You have done it all to yourself,
Which pleases me at this time.
I must laugh at it.
Everyman. You are delighted about this,

Om dat ghi mi van Gode hebt beroeft?
425 Hi is sot die eenich goet gheloeft.
Dat mach ic, Elckerlijc, wel beclaghen.
En wildi dan niet mede?
Tgoet. Ey seker, neen ick!
Elckerlijc. Och, wien sal ict dan claghen
Mede te gaen in desen groten last?
Eerst had ic op mijn Gheselscap ghepast;
430 Die seydt mi schoen toe menichfout,
Mer achter na sloech hi mi niet hout.
Daer vandic dattet al was bedroch.
Doen ghinc ic tot minen Maghen noch,
Die seydent mi toe, claer als ghelas.
435 Ten eynde vandic als ghedwas.
Doen wert ic dencken op mijn Goet;
Daer ic aen leyde minen moet.
Dat en gaf mi troest noch raet
Dan dattet Goet in verdoemenis staet.
440 Dies ic mi selven wel mach bespuwen.
Tfy, Elckerlijc, u mach wel gruwen!
Hoe deerlic mach ic u versmaden!
Heere God, wie sal mi nu beraden,
Daer ic noch bi werde verhuecht?
445 Niemant bat dan mijn Duecht.
Maer lazen! si is so teer van leden,
Ic meen, si niet connen en sou vander steden.
Och, en sal ic haer nyet toe dorren spreken?
Wil ic? neen ick; ick sal nochtans.
450 Tvare alst mach, ic moeter henen.
Waer sidi, mijn Duecht?
Duecht. Ick ligghe hier al verdwenen
Te bedde, vercrepelt ende al ontset.
Ick en kan gheroeren niet een let,
So hebdi mi gevoecht met uwen misdaden.
455 Wat is u ghelieven?
Elckerlijc. Ghi moet mi beraden,
Want icx noot heb tot mijnder vromen.
Duecht. Elckerlijc, ic heb wel vernomen
Dat ghi ter rekeninghen sijt ghedaecht
Voer den oversten Heere.
Elckerlijc. Och, dat si u gheclaecht!
460 Ick come u bidden uuttermaten
Dat ghi daer met mi gaet.

That you have robbed me of God?
425 He is foolish who trusts any goods.
I, Everyman, may well lament that.
You will not [go] with [me] then?
Goods.   Certainly not!
Everyman.   Oh, to whom shall I complain about this
To go with me in this great need?
First I had reckoned on Fellowship,
430 Who promised it handsomely to me often,
But afterwards he was not faithful to me.
Then I found that it was all deceit.
Then, moreover, I went to my kinsmen,
Who promised it to me clear as glass.
435 In the end I found [it to be] all talk.
Then I began to think of my Goods,
On which I had set my heart.
That [one] gave me no other help or counsel
Than that Goods has been damned.
440 Therefore I may well spit at myself.
Fie, Everyman, you may well shudder.
How utterly can I despise you!
Lord God, who will now assist me
By which I may still be gladdened?
445 No one better than my Virtue.
But, alas, she is so weak in the limbs,
I think she would not be able [to move] from the spot.
Ah, shall I not dare to speak to her?
Shall I? No! I shall nonetheless.
450 Fare as it may, I must [go] there.
Where are you, my Virtue?
Virtue.   I lie here all spent,
In bed, paralyzed and completely exhausted.
I cannot move a limb;
So you have made me with your misdeeds.
455 What do you want?
Everyman.   You must assist me,
For I need it for my benefit.
Virtue. Everyman, I have well understood
That you are summoned to [your] reckoning
Before the supreme Lord.
Everyman. Oh, about that I should like to complain to you.
460 I come to ask you urgently
That you go there with me.

Duecht.   Al mocht mi al die werelt baten,
Ick en konst niet alleen ghestaen.
Elckerlijc.   Ay lazen, sidi so cranck?
465 *Duecht.*   Dit hebdi mi al ghedaen.
Haddi mi volcomelijc ghevoecht,
Ic sou u rekeninghe, die nu onreyn is,
Ghesuvert hebben, des u siel in weyn is.
Siet u ghescrifte ende uwe wercken,
470 Hoe dat si hier legghen!
Elckerlijc.   Gods cracht wil mi stercken!
Men siet hier een letter niet die reyn es.
Is dit al mijn ghescrifte?
Duecht.   Seker, ick meens.
Dat moechdi sien aen mijn ghesonde.
Elckerlijc.   Mijn waerde Duecht, uut goeden gronde,
475 Ic bid u, troost mi tot mijnen orboren,
Oft ic bin eewelijc verloren.
Want Geselscap, Vrient, Maghe ende Goet
Sijn mi af ghegaen; in rechter oetmoet
Helpt mi mijn rekeninghe sluyten
480 Hier voer den hoochsten Heere.
Duecht.   Elckerlijc, ghi deert mi seere.
Ick sou u helpen waer icx machtich.
Elckerlijc.   Duecht, soudi mi wel beraden?
Duecht.   Dies bin ick bedachtich,
Hoe wel ic niet en mach vander steden,
485 Noch heb ic een suster, die sal gaen mede;
Kennisse heetse, die u leyden sal
Ende wijsen, hoemen u beraden sal
Te trecken ter rekeninghe, die fel es.
Kennisse.   Elckerlijc, ick sal u bewaren.
Elckerlijc.   Ick waen, mi nu wel es.
490 Ick ben een deels ghepayt van desen.
Gods lof moeter in gheeert wesen.
Duecht.   Als si u gheleyt heeft sonder letten,
Daer ghi u suveren sult van smetten,
Dan sal ic gesont werden ende comen u bij
495 Ende gaen ter rekeningen als Duecht mit di,
Om te helpen zommeren tot uwer vruecht
Voerden oversten Heere.
Elckerlijc.   Danck hebt, uutvercoren Duecht!
Ick bin ghetroost boven maten
Op u suete woerden.

Virtue. Even if I were to win the whole world,
I could not stand alone.
Everyman. Alas, are you so sick?
465 *Virtue.* This you have all done to me.
Had you completely followed my wishes,
I should have cleansed your reckoning,
Which is now unclean, because of which your soul is in sadness.
See your writings and your works,
470 How they lie here!
Everyman. May God's might strengthen me!
One does not see here a letter that is clean.
Is this all my writing?
Virtue. Certainly, I mean it!
That you may see from my health.
Everyman. My dear Virtue, with a sincere heart,
475 I beg you help me to my benefit,
Or I shall be eternally lost.
For Fellowship, Friend, Kinsman, and Goods
Have forsaken me; very humbly [I beg],
Help me to balance my reckoning
480 Here before the highest Lord.
Virtue. Everyman, I am deeply sorry for you.
I would help you were I able to [do] it.
Everyman. Virtue, would you indeed assist me?
Virtue. This I intend
Although I cannot [move] from the spot.
485 Yet I have a sister who will go with you;
Knowledge, she is called, who will guide you
And show you how one will assist you
To set forth to the reckoning, which is severe.
Knowledge. Everyman, I shall protect you.
Everyman. I think [it] is well with me now.
490 I am somewhat reassured by this.
God must be praised and honored by this.
Virtue. When she has led you without delay
Where you shall cleanse yourself from stains,
Then I shall become healthy and aid you
495 And go with you to the reckoning as Virtue,
To help you make [your] accounting, to your joy,
Before the supreme Lord.
Everyman. Thank you, Virtue elect.
I am comforted beyond measure
By your sweet words.

Kennisse.   Nu gaen wi ons saten
500 Tot Biechten; si es een suver rivier.
Sy sal u pureren.
Elckerlijc.   Uut reyner bestier
So gaen wi tot daer; ic bids u beyden.
W*a*er woent Biechte?
Kennisse.   Int Huys der Salicheden;
Daer sullen wijse vinden, soudic meenen.
505 *Elckerlijc.*   Ons Here God wil ons gracie verleenen
Tot haer, die ons vertroosten moet.
Kennisse.   Elckerlijc, dit is Biechte; valt haer te voet.
Sy es voer Gode lief ende waert.
Elckerlijc.   O gloriose bloome diet al verclaert
510 Ende doncker smetten doet vergaen,
Ick knyele voer u, wilt mi dwaen
Van mijnen sonden; in u aenscouwen
I*c*k coem met Kennisse te mijnen behouw*en*,
Bedroeft van herten ende seer vers*a*echt.
515 Want ic ben vander Doot ghedaecht
Te gaen een pelgrimagie, die groot *is.*
Oec moet ic rekening doe*n, alst* bloot is,
Voor Hem, die doersiet alle gronde.
Nu bid ic, Biechte, moeder van ghesonde:
520 Verclaert mijn brie*v*en, want Du*e*cht seer onghesont is.
Biechte.   Elckerlijc, u lijden mi wel kont is;
Om dat ghi mit Kennisse tot mi sijt comen,
So sal ic u troesten tuwer vromen.
Oec sal ic u gheven een juweelken rene,
525 Dat Penitencie heet alleene.
Daer suldi u lichaem mede termijnen
Met abstinencie ende met pijnen.
Hout daer, siet die gheesselen puere:
Dats Penitencie, strang ende suere.
530 Peyst dat ons Here oeck was geslaghen
Met geesselen, dat Hi woude verdraghen,
Recht voer Sijn pelgrimagie stranghe;
Kennisse, hout hem in desen ganghe;
So sal sijn Duecht werden spoedich.
535 Ende emmer hoept aen Gode oetmoedich,
Want u tijt varinck eynden sal.
Bidt Hem ghenade; dit suldi vinden al,
Ende orboert die harde knopen altijt.
Kennisse, siet dat ghi bi hem sijt,

Knowledge. Let us go now
500 To Confession; she is a clear river.
She will cleanse you.
Everyman.   With a pure intention
We shall go there; I beg it of you both.
Where does Confession live?
Knowledge.   In the House of Blessedness;
There we shall find her, I should think.
505 *Everyman.* Our Lord God may grant us grace
With her, who may comfort us.
Knowledge. Everyman, this is Confession; fall at her feet.
She is very dear and precious to God.
Everyman. O glorious flower that cleanses all
510 And makes dark stains disappear,
I kneel before you. Do wash me
Of my sins. In your sight
I come with Knowledge for my salvation,
Sad of heart and very fearful,
515 For I have been summoned by Death
To go [on] a pilgrimage that is great.
Also I must give a reckoning, *as it* is clear,
Before him, who penetrates all depths.
Now I beg, Confession, mother of health,
520 Cleanse my account, for Virtue is very sick.
Confession. Everyman, your suffering is well known to me.
Since you have come to me with Knowledge,
I shall help you to your benefit.
Also I shall give you a pure jewel
525 That is called penance only.
With that you shall chastise your body
By abstinence and mortification.
Take hold; see the pure scourge:
That's penance, hard and sour.
530 Remember that our Lord was also beaten
With scourges, which He was willing to endure,
Just before His hard pilgrimage.
Knowledge, keep him on this path;
Then his Virtue will get well.
535 And always humbly hope in God,
For soon your time shall end.
Beg of Him mercy; this you will find fully,
And always use the hard knots.
Knowledge, see that you are beside him

540   Als hi tot Penitencien keert.
     Kennisse.   Gaerne, Biechte.
     Elckerlijc.   God si hier in gheeert!
     Nu wil ic mijn penitencie beghinnen,
     Want dlicht heeft mi verlicht van binnen,
     Al sijn dese knopen strenghe ende hardt.
545   *Kennisse.*   Elckerlijc, hoe suer dat u wert,
     Siet dat ghi u penitencie volstaet.
     Ick, Kennisse, sal u gheven raet,
     Dat ghi u rekeninghe sult tonen bloot.
     Elckerlijc.   O levende Leven! o hemels Broot!
550   O Wech der waerheyt! o godlic Wesen,
     Die neder quam uut Sijns Vaders schoot
     In een suver Maecht gheresen,
     Om dat ghi Elckerlijc wout ghenesen,
     Die Adam onterfde bi Yeven rade.
555   O Heylighe Triniteyt uut ghelesen,
     Wilt mi vergheven mijn mesdade,
     Want ic begheer aen U ghenade.

     O godlijc Tresoer! o coninclijc Saet!
     O alder werelt toeverlaet!
560   Specie der engelen sonder versaden!
     Spiegel der vruecht daert al aen staet,
     Wiens licht Hemel ende aerde beslaet,
     Hoort mijn roepen, al yst te spade.
     Mijn bede wilt inden troen ontfaen.
565   Al bin ic sondich, mesdadich ende quaet,
     Scrijft mi int boeck des Hemels blade,
     Want ic begheer aen U ghenade.

     O Maria, moeder des Hemels almachtich!
     Staet mi ter noot bi voordachtich,
570   Dat mi die Viant niet en verlade!
     Want nakende is mi die Doot crachtich.
     Bidt voer mi dijnen Sone voerdachtich,
     So dat ic mach gaen inden rechten pade,
     Daer die wegen niet en sijn onrachtich.
575   Maect mi uwes Kints rijc delachtich,
     So dat ic in Sijn Passie bade,
     Want ic begheer aen U ghenade.

     Kennisse, gheeft mi die gheselen bi vramen,

540   When he turns to penance.
      Knowledge. Gladly, Confession.
      Everyman.   God be honored in this!
      Now I shall begin my penance.
      For the Light has lightened me within,
      Although these knots are harsh and hard.
545   *Knowledge.* Everyman, however sour it become to you,
      See that you carry out your penance.
      I, Knowledge, shall give you help,
      So that you can show your reckoning openly.
      Everyman. O living Life, O heavenly Bread!
550   O Way of Truth, O Divine Being,
      Who came down from out of His Father's lap,
      Descending into a pure maiden,
      Because Thou wanted to heal every man,
      Whom Adam disinherited by Eve's advice.
555   O Holy Trinity of eminent worth,
      Do forgive me my misdeeds,
      For I seek mercy from Thee.

      O divine Treasure, O kingly *Seed*,
      O Refuge of all the world,
560   Food of angels without satiety,
      Mirror of joy, on whom all depends,
      Whose light *occupies* Heaven and earth,
      Hear my crying although it is late;
      Receive my prayer at the throne.
565   Though I am sinful, wicked, and evil,
      Write me in the book of Heaven's sheet.
      For I seek mercy from Thee.

      O Mary, mother of almighty Heaven,
      Stand by me in need with concern
570   So that the Devil may not overmaster me,
      For mighty Death is approaching me.
      Pray for me with concern to thy Son,
      So that I can walk on the right path,
      Where the ways are not *crooked*.
575   Make me a sharer in the kingdom of thy Child
      So that I may bathe in His passion,
      For I seek mercy from thee.

      Knowledge, give me the scourge to [my] benefit,

Die Penitencie hieten bi namen,
580   Ic salt beghinnen, God geefs mi gracie.
    Kennisse.   Elckerlijc, God gheve u spacie!
    So ghevicx u inden naem ons Heeren,
    Daer ghi ter rekeninghe moet keeren.
    Elckerlijc.   Inden naem des Vaders ende des Soens, mede
585   Des Heylige Gheest, inder Drievuldichede,
    Beghin ic mijn penitencie te doen.
    Neemt, lichaem, voer dat ghi waert *so coen*
    Mij te bringhen inden wech der plaghen.
    Daer om moetti nu sijn gheslaghen.
590   Ghi hebbes wel verdient ghewarich.
    Ay broeders, waer soe mochti
    Door penitencie waen
    Tseghen dat ghi u *pelgrimaige* moet gaen,
    Die Elckerlijc moet nemen aen.
595   *Duecht.*   God danc! Ic beghin nu wel te gaen,
    Want Elckerlijc heeft mi ghenesen;
    Dies wil ic eewich bi hem wesen.
    Oeck sal ic sijn weldaet clareren; dies wil ic bi hem gaen te tijde.

    Kennisse.   Elckerlijc, sijt vro ende blijde!
600   U weldaet coemt, nu sijt verhuecht!
    Elckerlijc.   Wie maecht sijn, Kennisse?
    Kennisse.   Het is u Duecht,
    Gans ende ghesont op die beene.
    Elckerlijc.   Van blijscappen ic weene.
    Nu wil ic meer slaen dan te voren.
605   *Duecht.*   Elckerlijc, pelgrijm uutvercoren,
    Ghebenedijt sidi, sone der victorien,
    Want u is nakende dlicht der glorien.
    Ghi hebt mi ghemaect al ghesont;
    Des sal ic u bi bliven teewigher stont.
610   God sal dijnre ontfermen, hebt goet betrouwen.
    Elckerlijc.   Welcoem, Duecht; mijn oghen douwen
    In rechter oetmoedigher blijscap soet.
    Kennisse.   En slaet niet meer, hebt goeden moet.
    God siet u leven inden throone.
615   Doet aen dit cleet tuwen loone.
    Het is met uwen tranen bevloeyt;
    Dus draechtet vrij, onghemoeyt;
    Oft anders soudijt voor Gode gemissen.
    Elckerlijc.   Hoe heet dit cleet?

Which is called penance by name;
580 I shall begin [with] it; God give me grace to [do] it.
Knowledge. Everyman, may God give you time!
I then give it to you in the name of our Lord,
Where you must come to give reckoning.
Everyman. In the name of the Father and of the Son, also
585 Of the Holy Ghost, in the Trinity,
I begin to do my penance.
Take this, body, because you were *so bold*
[As] to lead me in the way of disaster.
Therefore you must now be beaten.
590 You have indeed truly deserved it.
O brothers, wherever you might
Wade through penance
Against [the time] that you must go [on] your *pilgrimage*,
Which Everyman has to undertake.
595 *Virtue.* Thank God, I now begin to move about well,
For Everyman has made me well;
Therefore I shall be with him for ever.
Also I shall testify to his good deeds; therefore I shall go
[with him at once.
Knowledge. Everyman, be merry and glad!
600 Your Good Deeds comes, now rejoice!
Everyman. Who can it be, Knowledge?
Knowledge.   It is your Virtue,
Whole and healthy on her legs.
Everyman. From joy I weep.
Now I will strike harder than before.
605 *Virtue.* Everyman, pilgrim elect,
Blessed be you, son of victory!
For to you the light of glory is coming.
You have made me completely well.
Therefore I shall remain with you for ever.
610 God will have mercy on you, rest assured.
Everyman. Welcome, Virtue. My eyes dew
In right humble, sweet joy.
Knowledge. Strike no more; be of good heart;
God on the throne sees you live.
615 Put on this garment as your reward.
It is wet with your tears;
So wear it freely, *unhindered*;
Otherwise you would miss it before God.
Everyman. What is this garment called?

Kennisse.   Tcleet van berouwenissen.

620 Het sal Gode alte wel behaghen.

Duecht.   Elckerlijc, wilt dat cleet aendrag*h*en,

Want Kennisse hevet u aenghedaen.

Elckerlijc.   Soe wil ic berouwenisse ontfaen,

Om dat God dit cleet heeft so weert.

625 Nu willen wi gaen onverveert.

Duecht, hebdi ons rekeninghe claer?

Duecht.   Jae ick, Elckerlijc.

Elckerlijc.   So en heb ic ghenen vaer.

Op, vrienden; en wilt van mi niet sceyden!

Kennisse.   Neen wi, Elckerlijc.

Duecht.   Ghi moet noch met u leyden

630 Drie personen van groter macht.

Elckerlijc.   Wie souden si wesen?

Duecht.   Wijsheyt ende u Cracht;

U Schoonheit en mach niet achter bliven.

Kennisse.   Noch moetti hebben sonder becliven

U Vijf Sinnen als u beraders.

635 *Elckerlijc.*   Hoe soude icxse ghecrighen.

Kennisse.   Roepse alle gader.

Si sullent hooren al sonder verdrach.

Elckerlijc.   Mijn vrienden, coemt alle op mijnen dach!

Wijsheyt, Cracht, Schoonheyt, ende Vijf Sinnen!

Cracht.   Hier sijn wi alle tot uwer minnen.

640 Wat wildi van ons hebben ghedaen?

Duecht.   Dat ghi met Elckerlijc wilt gaen

Sijn pelgrimagie helpen volbringhen,

Want hi gedaecht is ter rekeningen

Voor Gode te comen onghelet.

645 Siet oft ghi mede wilt.

Schoonheyt.   Wi willen alle met,

Tsijnre hulpen ende tsijnen rade.

Vroetscap.   Dat willen wi certeyn.

Elckerlijc.   O almoghende God, ghenade!

U love ic dat ic dus heb ghebracht

Vroescap, Scoonheyt, Vijf Sinnen ende Cracht,

650 Ende mijn Duecht met Kennisse claer.

Nu heb ic gheselscap te wille daer;

Ic en geerder niet meer te minen verdoene.

Cracht.   Ick blive u bi, sto*u*t ende koene,

Al waert te gaen in eenen strijt.

655 *Vijf Sinnen.*   Ende ic, al waert die werelt wijt.

Knowledge.   The garment of contrition.
620 It will please God very well.
Virtue. Everyman, wear this garment,
For Knowledge has put it on you.
Everyman. So I will receive contrition
Because God values this garment so highly.
625 Now let us go without fear.
Virtue, have you our reckoning pure?
Virtue. Yes, Everyman.
Everyman.   Then I have no fear.
Up, friends; do not part from me.
Knowledge. No, Everyman.
Virtue.   Yet you must take with you
630 Three persons of great power.
Everyman. Who should they be?
Virtue.   Wisdom and your Strength;
Your Beauty may not stay behind.
Knowledge. Yet you must have without delay
Your Five Senses as your assistants.
635 *Everyman.* How should I acquire them?
Knowledge.   Call them all.
They will hear it quite without delay.
Everyman. My friends, come all on my day!
Wisdom, Strength, Beauty, and Five Senses!
Strength. Here we are, all of us, at your service.
640 What would you have us do?
Virtue. That you would go with Everyman.
To help [him] perform his pilgrimage.
For he has been summoned to come
At once before God *for the reckoning.*
645 See whether you want to come with him.
Beauty.   We will all [go] with [him]
To help him and assist him.
Prudence. That we will certainly [do].
Everyman.   O almighty God, mercy!
Thee I praise that I have thus brought along
Prudence, Beauty, Five Senses, and Strength
650 And my Virtue and pure Knowledge.
Now I have company *here* according to my wish.
I wish no more of it for my need.
Strength. I shall remain with you, bold and courageous,
Even if it were to go into a battle.
655 *Five Senses.* And I, although it were the wide world,

Ic en scheyde van u in gheenre noot.

Schoonheyt. So en sal ic oeck tot in die doot,

Comer af datter af comen mach!

Vroetscap. Elckerlijc, wes ic u doe ghewach,

660 Gaet voersienich ende al met staden.

Wi sullen u alle duecht raden

Ende sullen u helpen wel bestieren.

Elckerlijc. Dit sijn die vrienden die niet en faelgieren.

Dat lone hem God, die hemelsche Vader!

665 Nu hoort, mijn vrienden, alle gader:

Ick wil gaen stellen mijn testament

Voor u allen hier in present.

In caritaten ende in rechter oetmoe*de*

Deel ic den armen van mijnen goede

670 Deen helft, ende dander helft daer nae

Ghevick daer si schuldich is te gaen.

Dit doen ic den Viant nu te schanden,

Om los te gaen uut sinen handen.

Nae mijn leven in *desen* daghe.

675 *Kennisse.* Elckerlijc, hoort wat ick ghewaghe:

Gaet totten priesterliken staet

Ende siet dat ghi van hem ontfaet

Tsacrament ende Olijs mede.

Dan keert hier weder tot deser stede.

680 Wi sullen alle nae u verbeyden.

Vijf Sinnen. Jae, Elckerlijc, gaet u bereyden.

Ten is keyser, coninc, hertoghe of grave,

Die van Gode hebben alsulcken *gave*,

Als die minste priester doet alleene.

685 Van alden sacramenten reene

Draecht hi den slotel al doer bereyt

Tot des menschen salicheyt,

Die ons God teender medicijne

Gaf uuter herten Sijne

690 Hier in desen aertschen leven.

Die Heylighe Sacramenten seven:

Doopsel, Vormsel, Priesterscap goet

Ende tSacrament, God Vleesch ende Bloet,

Huwelic ende tHeylich Olyzel met——

695 Dit zijn die seven onbesmet

Sacramenten van groter waerden.

Elckerlijc. Ic wil Gods lichaem minlic aenvaerden

Ende oetmoedelijc totten priester gaen.

I shall not part from you in any distress.
Beauty. Neither shall I till death,
Come of it what may come of it!
Prudence. Everyman, [listen to] what I say:
660 Go with foresight and quite calmly.
We shall counsel you all virtue
And shall help to guide you well.
Everyman. These are the friends who do not fail;
May God reward them, the heavenly Father.
665 Now listen, all my friends:
I will go to make my will
Before you all here present.
In charity and true humility
I deal out to the poor of my goods
670 One half, and the other half thereafter
I assign where it by rights should go.
This I do now to shame the Devil,
To get out of his hands
After my life on *this* day.
675 *Knowledge*. Everyman, listen to what I say:
Go to the priesthood
And see that you receive from them
The Sacrament and also Oil.
Then come back here to this place.
680 We shall all wait for you.
Five Senses. Yes, Everyman, go prepare yourself.
There is no emperor, king, duke or count
Who holds from God such a gift
As does the least priest alone.
685 Of all the pure sacraments
He bears the key, ever ready
For the salvation of mankind,
Which God for a medicine
Gave us out of His heart
690 Here, in this earthly life.
The seven Holy Sacraments——
Baptism, Confirmation, Priesthood good,
And the Sacrament —— God, flesh and blood ——
Matrymony, and the Holy Oil also——
695 These are the seven undefiled
Sacraments of great price.
Everyman. I will receive God's body with love
And go humbly to the priest.

Vijf Sinnen.   Elckerlijc, dat is wel ghedaen.
700 God laet u met salicheden volbringhen!
Die priester gaet boven alle dinghen.
Si zijn die ons die Scriftuere leeren
Ende den mensche van sonden keeren.
God heeft hem meer machts ghegheven
705 Dan den ynghelen int eewich leven.
Want elc priester kan maken claer
Met vijf woerden opten outaer
Inder missen——des zijt vroet——
Gods lichaem, warachtich Vleesch ende Bloet,
710 Ende handelt den Scepper tusscen zijn handen.
Die priester bint ende ontbint alle banden
Inden hemel ende opter aerde.
Och edel priester van groter waerde,
Al custen wi u voetstappen, gi waret waert!
715 Wie van sonden troost begaert
Die en connen vinden gheen toeverlaet
Dan aenden priesterliken staet.
Dit heeft die Heere den priester ghegheven
Ende zijn in Zijn stede hier ghebleven.
720 Dus zijn si boven die enghelen gheset.
Kennisse.   Dats waer, diet wel hout onbesmet.
Mer doen Hi hinc met groter smerten
Aent cruce, daer gaf Hij ons uut Zijnder herten
Die seven Sacramenten met seere;
725 Hi en vercoft ons niet, die Heere!
Hier om dat Sinte Peter lijdt
Dat si alle zijn vermaledijt
Die God copen oft vercopen
Ende daer af ghelt nemen met hoopen.
730 Si gheven den sondaer quaet exempel;
Haer kinder lopen inden tempel
Ende som sitten si bi wiven
In onsuverheyt van liven.
Dese zijn emmers haers sins onvroet.
735 *Vijf Sinnen.*   Ic hope, of God wil, dat niemant en doet.
Daer om laet ons die priesters eeren
Ende volghen altijt haer leeren.
Wi zijn haer scapen ende si ons herden,
Daer wi alle in behoet werden.
740 Laet dit wesen niet meer vermaen.
Duecht.   Elckerlijc coemt; hi heeft voldaen.

Five Senses. Everyman, that is well done.

700 May God let you perform it for [your] salvation!
The priest surpasses all things:
They are [the ones] who teach us Scripture
And turn man from sins.
God has given them more power

705 Than the angels in eternal life,
For every priest can make manifest
With five words on the altar
In the Mass——be sure about this——
God's body, true flesh and blood,

710 And holds his Creator between his hands.
The priest binds and unbinds all bonds
In heaven and on earth.
O noble priest of great worth,
Even though we kissed your footsteps, you would deserve it.

715 Who desires release from sins,
These can find no refuge
Except in the priesthood.
This the Lord has given to the priest,
And [they] have stayed here in His place.

720 Thus they are set above the angels.
Knowledge. That's true [for him] who keeps it undefiled.
But when He hung with great pain
On the cross, there He gave us from his heart
The seven sacraments with pain.

725 He did not sell them to us, the Lord.
Therefore Saint Peter declares
That they are all accursed
Who buy or sell God
And make heaps of money out of it.

730 They give the sinner a bad example;
Their children walk in the temple
And sometimes sit with women
In impurity of living.
These have in any case lost their senses.

735 *Five Senses*. I hope, if God wills, that no one does.
Therefore let us honor the priests
And always follow their teaching.
We are their sheep and they our shepherds,
By whom we are all protected.

740 Let this be sufficient warning.
Good Deeds. Everyman comes; he has settled up.

Dus laet ons zijn op ons hoede.
Elckerlijc.   Heer God, mi is so wel te moede,
Dat ic van vruechden wene als een kint.
745 Ic hebbe ontfaen mijn sacrament
Ende dat Olizel mede; danc heb diet riet.
Nu vrienden, sonder te letten yet,
Ick danck Gode dat ic u allen vant.
Slaet aen dit roeyken alle u hant
750 Ende volghet mi haestelic na desen.
Ick gae vore, daer ic wil wesen.
Ons Heere God, wil mi gheleyden.
Cracht.   Elckerlijc, wi en willen van u niet sceyden,
Voer ghi ghedaen hebt dese vaert.
755 *Vroetscap.*   Wi blivens u bi onghespaert
Also wi gheloeft *hebben* oec langhe.
Kennisse.   Och, dits een pelgrimagie seer strange,
Die Elckerlijc sal moeten gaen.
Cracht.   Elckerlijc, siet hoe wi u bi staen,
760 Sterck, vroem; en hebt gheen vaer.
Elckerlijc.   Ay mi! die leden zijn mi so swaer
Dat si gaen beven voer den gru.
Lieve vrienden, wi en willen niet keeren nu.
Sal ic mijn pelgrimagie betalen,
765 So moet ic hier binnen dalen
In desen put ende werden aerde.
Schoonheyt.   Wat! in desen putte?
Elckerlijc.   Ja, van deser waerden.
Soe moeten wi werden, clein ende groot.
Schoonheyt.   Wat! hier in versmoren?
Elckerlijc.   Ja, hier in versmoren ende bliven doot
770 Ter werelt, mer levende wesen altijt
Voerden oversten Heere.
Schoonheyt.   Ick schelt u al quijt.
Adieu! vaert wel! ic schoer mijn scout.
Elckerlijc.   Wat, Schoonheyt?
Schoonheyt.   Ic bin al dove; ic en saghe niet omme
775 Al mocht mi baten alder werelt schat.
Elckerlijc.   Waer op wil ic mi verlaten?
Schoonheyt vliet, oftmense jaechde.
Nochtan te voren, doen ic haer vraechde,
Woude si met mi sterven ende leven.
780 *Cracht.*   Elckerlijc, ic wil u oec begheven.
U spel en behaecht mi niet te deghe.

Let us therefore be on our guard.
Everyman. Lord God, I am in such a benign mood
That I weep for joy like a child.
745 I have received my sacrament
And the Oil also; thanks to him who advised it.
Now, friends, without any tarrying,
I thank God that I found you all.
Lay all [of you] your hands on this little cross
750 And quickly follow me after this.
I will lead [the way] to where I want to be.
Our Lord God, may Thou guide me.
Strength. Everyman, we shall not part from you
Before you have made this journey.
755 *Prudence*. In respect to it we will remain with you
As we have indeed long promised.
Knowledge. Oh, this is a very hard pilgrimage
On which Everyman has to go.
Strength. Everyman, see how we stand by you,
760 Strong, brave; have no fear.
Everyman. Alas, my limbs are so heavy
That they begin *to tremble* from horror.
Dear friends, we will not return now.
If I am to complete my pilgrimage,
765 Then I must go down here
Into this pit and become earth.
Beauty. What, into this pit?
Everyman.   Yes, such stuff
We must become, low and high.
Beauty. What, smother in here?
Everyman. Yes, here to smother and die
770 In the world, but be alive for ever
Before the supreme Lord.
Beauty.   I take back from you what I said.
Adieu! Farewell! I retract my promise.
Everyman. What, Beauty?
Beauty.   I am quite deaf; I should not look back
775 Though all the world's treasure could benefit me.
Everyman. In what shall I trust?
Beauty flees as if chased away.
Still, when I asked her earlier,
She would die and live with me.
780 *Strength*. Everyman, I shall also leave you.
Your game does not altogether please me.

Elckerlijc.   Cracht, suldi mi oec ontgaen?
Cracht.   Ja, ic wil seker weghe.
Daer mede ghesloten, een voer al.
Elckerlijc.   Lieve Cracht, ontbeyt noch!
Cracht.   Bi Sinte Loy, ick en sal!
785 Waendi dat ic in dien put wil versmoren?
Elckerlijc.   En*de* suldi mi dan ontgaen?
Cracht.   Ja ick, tes al verloren,
Al soudi uwen navel uut crijten.
Elckerlijc.   Suldi aldus u ghelofte quijten?
Ghi soudt mi bi bliven, so ghi seyt.
790 *Cracht.*   Ick heb u verre ghenoech gheleyt.
Oec sidi oudt ghenoech, ic waen,
U pelgrimagie alleen te gaen.
Mi es leet dat icker heden quam.
Elckerlijc.   Ay, lieve Cracht, ic make u gram.
795 *Cracht.*   Tes al verloren; rust u hoeft
Ende gaet int doncker huys.
Elckerlijc.   Dit en had ic u niet gheloeft.
Wie wil hem verlaten op zijn cracht?
Si vliet alst mist doet uuter gracht.
Schoonheit is als wint die vlieghet.
800 Ay, getrouwe vrienden, dat ghi dus lieget!
Ghi seydet mi toe schoon ter kore.
Vroetschap.   Elckerlijc, ic wil oeck gaen dore
Ende nemen uutstel van desen.
Waendi dat wi hier in willen wesen?
805 Hoet u van dien, ic wils mi wachten.
Elckerlijc.   O Vroetschap, Vroetschap!
Vroeschap.   Ick en wil niet mede.
Tes verloren ghevroescapt, claer.
Elckerlijc.   Lieve Vroeschap, coemt doch soe nae
Dat ghi hier binnen den gront aensiet.
810 Ick bidts u oetmoedelijc.
Vroeschap.   Bi Sinte Loy, ick en doe des niet!
Mi rouwet dat icker ye quam so bi.
Elckerlijc.   Och, al mist dat God niet en si!
Schoonheyt, Cracht ende Vroescap groot,
Het vliet van Elckerlijc als coemt de doot.
815 Arm mensche, waer sal ic nu op lenen?
Vijf Sinnen.   Elckerlijc, ic wil oec henen
Ende volghen den anderen die u ontwerven.
Elckerlijc.   Och, lieve Vijf Sinnen!

Everyman. Strength, will you also leave me?
Strength.　　　　　Yes, I certainly shall away;
There is an end of it, once and for all.
Everyman. Dear Strength, please wait!
Strength.　　　　　By Saint Loy, I will not!
785　Do you think that I want to smother in that pit?
Everyman. Will you leave me then?
Strength.　　　　　Yes, it's all lost
Even though you should cry till your navel burst.
Everyman. Will you thus redeem your promise?
You would stay with me, so you said.
790　*Strength*. I have guided you far enough.
Besides, you are old enough, I think,
To go [on] your pilgrimage alone.
I am sorry that I came here now.
Everyman. Alas, dear Strength, I am making you angry.
795　*Strength*. It's quite useless; rest your head
And go into the dark house.
Everyman. This I should not have believed of you.
Who shall trust in his Strength?
He flees as mist does from the ditch.
Beauty is like wind that flies!
800　Alas, trusty friends, that you thus lie!
You very duly promised it to me.
Prudence. Everyman, I will also go away
And put off this.
Do you think that we want to be in here?
805　Beware of that; I will not do it.
Everyman. O Prudence, Prudence!
Prudence.　　　　　I will not [go] with [you].
Clearly, it's useless [to cry] "Prudence."
Everyman. Dear Prudence, come at least so near
That you see herein the bottom;
810　I humbly beg this of you.
Prudence.　　　　　By Saint Loy, I will not do this;
I am sorry that I ever came so near there.
Everyman. Oh, all that is not God fails!
Beauty, Strength, Prudence great,
It flies from Everyman when Death comes.
815　Poor man, on whom shall I now lean?
Five Senses. Everyman, I will also leave
And follow the others who turn away from you.
Everyman.　　　　　Oh, dear Five Senses!

Vijf Sinnen.   Ick en wil daer niet aen winnen.
Dat ghi veel roept, ten mach nyet baten.
820 *Elckerlijc.*   Och, suldi mi alle gader laten?
Duecht.   Neen wi, Elckerlijc; zijt ghestelt.
Elckerlijc.   Ay mi, mijn Vijf Sinnen!
Vijf Sinnen.   Roept al dat ghi wilt;
Ghi en sult mi niet meer van voor bekijken.
Elckerlijc.   Lieve Duecht, blijft ghi bi mi?
Duecht.   Ick en sal u nemmermeer beswijken,
825 Om leven, om sterven, of om gheen torment.
Elckerlijc.   Hier zijn ghetrouwe vrienden bekent!
Alle die mi ontgaen ghemeene,
Die mindic meer dan mijn Duecht alleene.
Kennisse, suldi mi oec begheven?
830 *Kennisse.*   Ja ic, Elckerlijc, als ghi eyndet u leven,
Mer seker niet eer, om gheen dangier.
Elckerlijc.   Danc hebt, Kennisse.
Kennisse.   Ick en scheyde niet van hier,
Voer dat ghi zijt daer ghi behoort.
Elckerlijc.   Mi dunct, wacharmen, wij moeten voert,
835 Rekeninghe doen ende ghelden mijn scult.
Want mijn tijt is schier vervult.
Neemter exempel aen diet hoort ende siet,
Ende merct hoet nu al van mi vliet;
Sonder mijn Duecht wil met mi varen.
840 *Duecht.*   Alle aertsche dinghen zijn al niet.
Elckerlijc.   Doch merct hoet nu al van mi vliet!
Duecht.   Schoonheyt, Cracht, Vroescap, dat hem liet,
Tgheselscap, die Vrienden ende Magen waren.
Elckerlijc.   Nu merct hoet nu al van mi vliet!
845 Sonder mijn Duecht, die wil mit mi varen.
Ghenade, Coninc der enghelen scharen!
Ghenade, Moeder Gods, staet mi bi!
Duecht.   Ic sal mi puer voer Gode verclaren.
Elckerlijc.   Ghenade, Coninc der enghelen scharen!
850 *Duecht.*   Cort ons die pine sonder verswaren.
Maect ons deynde los ende vri.
Elckerlijc.   Ghenade, Coninck der enghelen scharen!
Ghenade, Moeder Gods, staet mi bi!
In Uwen handen, Vader, hoe dat si,
855 Beveel ic u minen gheest in vreden.
Ick vare metter Duecht.
Kennisse.   Hi heeft leden dat wij alle moeten gelden.

Five Senses. I will not gain anything [by this journey].
That you cry [so] much will be no use.

820 *Everyman*. Oh, shall you all leave me?
Virtue. No, Everyman; be reassured.
Everyman. Alas, my Five Senses!
Five Senses.   Cry all that you want;
You will not look at me in front any more.
Everyman. Dear Virtue, will you stay with me?
Virtue.   I shall never leave you in the lurch

825 For life, for death, or for any torment.
Everyman. Here faithful friends are known!
All those who together leave me,
I loved them more than my Virtue alone.
Knowledge, will you also leave me?

830 *Knowledge*. Yes, Everyman, when you end your life,
But certainly not before, for no difficulty.
Everyman. Thank you, Knowledge.
Knowledge.   I shall not depart from here
Before you are where you belong.
Everyman. I think, alas, we must go on,

835 To give reckoning and pay my debt,
For my time is almost fulfilled.
Take example *from this* who hear and see this,
And mark how it all flees from me now.
Only my Virtue will go with me.

840 *Virtue*. All earthly things are altogether nothing.
Everyman. *But* mark how it all flees from me now.
Virtue. Beauty, Strength, Prudence, that deserted him,
Fellowship, who were friends and kinsmen.
Everyman. Now mark how it all flees from me now

845 Except my Virtue, who will go with me.
Mercy, King of hosts of angels!
Mercy, mother of God, stand by me!
Virtue. I shall appear pure before God.
Everyman. Mercy, King of hosts of angels!

850 *Virtue*. Shorten for us the pain without worsening [it].
Make the end for us light and free.
Everyman. Mercy, King of hosts of angels!
Mercy, mother of God, stand by me.
Into Thy hands, Father, however it be,

855 I commend to you my spirit in peace.
I go with Virtue.
Knowledge. He has undergone what we all must pay.

Die Duecht sal nu haer selven melden
Voer Hem diet al ordelen sal.
860 Mi dunct, ic hore der enghelen gheschal
Hier boven; den Hemel is seker ontdaen,
Daer Elckerlijc binnen sal zijn ontfaen.
Die Ynghel Seyt.   Coemt, uutvercoren bruyt,
Hier boven, ende hoort dat suete gheluyt
865 Der engelen mits uwe goede virtuyt.
Die siele neem ick den lichaem uut.
Haer rekeninghe is puer ende reyne.
Nu voer icse in des Hemels pleyne,
Daer wi alle moeten ghemeene
870 In comen, groot ende cleene.

Amen.

Die Naeprologhe

Neemt in dancke, cleyn ende groot,
Ende siet hoe Elckerlijc coemt *ter* doot.
Gheselscap, Vrienden ende Goet
Gaet Elckerlijc af; zijt des vroet.
875 Scoonheyt, Cracht, Vroescap ende Vijf Sinnen,
Tes al verganclijc; zijt des te binnen.
Sonder die Duecht volcht voer al.
Mer als die Duecht is so smal
Dat si niet mede en mach oft en kan,
880 Arm Elckerlijc, hoe vaerdi dan
Ter rekeninghen *voer* onsen Heere?
Dan gadi van wee, van seere.
Want na die Doot eest quaet te verhalen;
Daer en baet voerspraec noch talen.
885 Ay Elckerlijc, hoe moechdi wesen
Hovaerdich, nidich! seer uut ghelesen,
Merct desen spieghel, hebten voer oghen
Ende wilt u van hovardien poghen,
Ende oec van allen sonden met.
890 Nu laet ons bidden onghelet
Dat dit elck mensche moet vesten,
Dat wi voer Gode suver comen ten lesten.

Virtue will now herself report
Before Him who shall judge it all.
860 I think I hear the flourish of angels
Here above; Heaven has certainly been opened,
Wherein Everyman will be received.
The angel says: Come, chosen bride,
Here above, and hear the sweet sound
865 Of the angels because of your good Virtue.
The soul I take out of the body.
Her reckoning is pure and clean.
Now I lead her into the plain of Heaven,
Where we all together may
870 Enter, high and low.

Amen.

The Epilogue

Take it willingly, low and high,
And see how Everyman dies.
Fellowship, Friends, and Goods
Desert Everyman; be sure about this.
875 Beauty, Strength, Prudence, and Five Senses——
It's all transient; bear this in mind.
Only. Virtue follows before all others.
But when Virtue is so weak
That she may or cannot [come] along,
880 Poor Everyman, how shall you go then
To the reckoning *before* our Lord?
Then you will perish of woe, of pain,
For after death it is hard to make good;
There neither intercession nor pleading avail.
885 Ah, Everyman, how can you be
Proud, envious! Very esteemed [audience],
Mark this mirror; hold it before [your] eyes,
And stay away from pride
And also from all sins as well.
890 Now let us pray at once
That this [mirror] may so strengthen every man
That we come pure before God at last.

Des gonne ons die hemelsche Vader.
Amen segghet alle gader.

God heb lof!

Gheprent Tantwerpen buyten dye camer poorte inden gulden eenhoren
bij mi Willem vorsterman.

May the heavenly Father grant us this.
Say Amen all together.

God be praised!

Printed in Antwerp outside the Brewer Gate in the Golden Unicorn by me, William Vorsterman.

Everyman

Here beginneth a treatise how the hie Fader of Heven sendeth Dethe
to somon every creature to come and give acounte of their lives in this
worlde, and is in maner of a morall playe.

Messenger. I pray you all give your audience
    And here this mater with reverence,
    By figure a morall playe.
    The Somoninge of Everyman called it is,
5   That of our lives and endinge shewes
    How transitory we be all daye.
    This mater is wonder[ou]s precious,
    But the entent of it is more gracious
    And swete to bere awaye.
10   The story saith: Man, in the beginninge
    Loke well and take good heed to the endinge,
    Be you never so gay!
    Ye thinke sinne in the beginninge full swete,
    Whiche in the ende causeth the soule to wepe
15   Whan the body lieth in claye.
    Here shall you se how Felawship and Jolite,
    Bothe Strengthe, Pleasure, and Beaute,
    Will fade from the[e] as floure in Maye,
    For ye shall here how our Heven Kinge
20   Calleth Everyman to a generall rekeninge.
    Give audience and here what he doth saye.

God speketh.

God. I perceive, here in my majeste,
    How that all creatures be to me unkinde,
    Livinge without drede in worldely prosperite.
25   Of ghostly sight the people be so blinde,
    Drowned in sinne, they know me not for their God.
    In worldely riches is all their minde;
    They fere not my rightwisnes, the sharpe rod.
    My lawe that I shewed whan I for them died

30 They forgete clene, and shedinge of my blode rede.
    I hanged bitwene two *theves*, it cannot be denied;
    To gete them life I suffred to be deed;
    I heled their fete; with thornes hurt was my heed.
    I coude do no more than I dide, truely;
35 And nowe I se the people do clene forsake me.
    They use the seven deedly sinnes dampnable,
    As Pride, Coveitise, Wrath, and Lechery
    Now in the worlde be made commendable;
    And thus they leve of aungelles the hevenly company.
40 Every man liveth so after his owne pleasure,
    And yet of their life they be nothinge sure.
    I se the more that I them forbere
    The worse they be fro yere to yere.
    All that liveth appaireth faste;
45 Therfore I will, in all the haste,
    Have a rekeninge of every mannes persone,
    For, and I leve the people thus alone
    In their life and wicked tempestes,
    Verily they will become moche worse than beestes;
50 For now one wolde by envy another up ete;
    Charite they do all clene forgete.
    I hoped well that every man
    In my glory sholde make his mansion,
    And therto I had them all electe,
55 But now I se, like traitours dejecte,
    They thanke me not for the pleasure that I to them ment,
    Nor yet for their beinge that I them have lent.
    I profered the people grete multitude of mercy,
    And fewe there be that asketh it hertly.
60 They be so combred with worldly riches
    That nedes on them I must do justice,
    On every man livinge, without fere.
    Where arte thou, Deth, thou mighty messengere?

Dethe. Almighty God, I am here at your will,
65 Your commaundement to fulfill.

God. Go thou to Everyman
    And shewe him, in my name,
    A pilgrimage he must on him take
    Whiche he in no wise may escape,
70 And that he bringe with him a sure rekeninge

Without delay or ony taryenge.

Dethe. Lorde, I will in the worlde go renne over all
And cruelly out-serche both grete and small.
Every man will I beset that liveth beestly
75   Out of Goddes lawes and dredeth not foly.
He that loveth richesse I will strike with my darte,
His sight to blinde, and fro Heven to departe——
Excepte that almes be his good frende——
In Hell for to dwell, worlde without ende.
80   Loo, yonder I see Everyman walkinge.
Full litell he thinketh on my cominge;
His minde is on flesshely lustes and his treasure,
And grete paine it shall cause him to endure
Before the Lorde, Heven Kinge.
85   Everyman, stande still! Whider arte thou goinge
Thus gaily? Hast thou thy Maker forgete?

Everyman. Why askest thou?
Woldest thou wete?

Dethe. Ye[a], sir, I will shewe you:
90   In grete hast[e] I am sende to the[e]
Fro God out of His mageste.

Everyman. What, sente to me?

Dethe. Ye[a], certainly.
Thoughe thou have forgete Him here,
95   He thinketh on the[e] in the hevenly sp[h]ere,
As, or we departe, thou shalte knowe.

Everyman. What desireth God of me?

Dethe. That shall I shewe the[e]:
A rekeninge he will nedes have
100   Without ony lenger respite.

Everyman. To give a rekeninge longer laiser I crave;
This blinde mater troubleth my witte.

Dethe. On the[e] thou must take a longe journey;
Therfore thy boke of counte with the[e] thou bringe,

105   For turne againe thou can not by no waye.
          And loke thou be sure of thy rekeninge,
          For before God thou shalte answere and shewe
          Thy many badde dedes and good but a fewe;
          How thou hast spente thy life, and in what wise,
110   Before the chefe Lorde of Paradise.
          Have *a*do we were in that waye,
          For wete thou well thou shalte make none attournay.

Everyman. Full unredy I am suche rekeninge to give.
          I knowe the[e] not. What messenger arte thou?

115 *Dethe.* I am Dethe that no man dredeth,
          For every man I reste and no man spareth;
          For it is Goddes commaundement
          That all to me sholde be obedient.

Everyman. O Deth, thou comest whan I had the[e] leest in minde!
120   In thy power it lieth me to save;
          Yet of my good wil I give the[e] if thou wil be kinde;
          Ye[a], a thousande pounde shalte thou have——
          And differe this mater till another daye.

Dethe.   Everyman, it may not be by no waye.
125   I set not by golde, silver, nor richesse,
          Ne by pope, emperour, kinge, duke, ne princes,
          For, and I wolde receive giftes grete,
          All the worlde I might gete,
          But my custome is clene contrary.
130   I give the[e] no respite. Come hens and not tary!

Everyman. Alas, shall I have no lenger respite?
          I may saye Deth geveth no warninge!
          To thinke on the[e] it maketh my herte seke,
          For all unredy is my boke of rekeninge.
135   But xii. yere and I might have abidinge,
          My countinge-boke I wolde make so clere
          That my rekeninge I sholde not nede to fere.
          Wherfore, Deth, I praye the[e], for Goddes mercy,
          Spare me till I be provided of remedy!

140 *Dethe.* The[e] availeth not to crye, wepe, and praye,
          But hast[e] the[e] lightly that thou were gone that journaye

And preve thy frendes if thou can,
For wete thou well the tide abideth no man,
And in the worlde eche livinge creature
145   For Adam's sinne must die of nature.

Everyman. Dethe, if I sholde this pilgrimage take
And my rekeninge suerly make,
Shewe me, for saint charite,
Sholde I not come againe shortly?

150 *Dethe.* No, Everyman. And thou be ones there,
Thou mayst nevermore come here,
Trust me verily.

Everyman. O gracious God in the hie sete celestiall,
Have mercy on me in this moost nede!
155   Shall I have no company fro this vale terestriall
Of mine acquein*taun*ce, that way me to lede?

Dethe. Ye[a], if ony be so hardy
That wolde go with the[e] and bere the[e] company.
Hie the[e] that thou were gone to Goddes magnificence,
160   Thy rekeninge to give before His presence.
What, wenest thou thy live is given the[e]
And thy worldely gooddes also?

Everyman. I had wende so, verile.

Dethe. Nay, nay, it was but lende the[e].
165   For, as soone as thou arte go,
Another a while shall have it and than go therfro,
Even as thou hast done.
Everyman, thou arte mad! Thou hast thy wittes five,
And here on erthe will not amende thy live,
170   For sodeinly I do come.

Everyman. O wretched caitife, wheder shall I flee
That I might scape this endles sorowe?
Now, gentill Deth, spare me till to-morowe
That I may amende me
175   With good advisement.

Dethe. Naye, therto I will not consent,

Nor no man will I respite,
But to the herte sodeinly I shall smite
Without ony advisement.
180 And now out of thy sight I will me hi[e].
Se thou make the[e] redy shortely,
For thou mayst saye this is the daye
That no man livinge may scape awaye.

Everyman. Alas, I may well wepe with sighes depe!
185 Now have I no maner of company
To helpe me in my journey and me to kepe,
And also my writinge is full unredy.
How shall I do now for to excuse me?
I wolde to God I had never begete!
190 To my soule a full grete profite it had be,
For now I fere paines huge and grete.
The time passeth. Lorde, helpe, that all wrought!
For though I mourne, it availeth nought.
The day passeth and is almoost ago;
195 I wote not well what for to do.
To whome were I best my complaint to make?
What and I to Felawship therof spake
And shewed him of this sodeine chaunce?
For in him is all mine affiaunce.
200 We have in the worlde so many a daye
Be good frendes in sporte and playe.
I se him yonder, certainely.
I trust that he will bere me company;
Therfore to him will I speke to ese my sorowe.
205 Well mette, good Felawship, and good morowe!
Felawship speketh..
Felawship. Everyman, good morowe, by this daye!
Sir, why lokest thou so piteously?
If ony thinge be amisse, I praye the[e] me saye,
That I may helpe to remedy.

210 *Everyman.* Ye[a], good Felawship, ye[a],
I am in greate jeoparde.

Felawship. My true frende, shewe to me your minde.
I will not forsake the[e] to my lives ende
In the waye of good company.
215 *Everyman.* That was well spoken and lovingly.

Felawship. Sir, I must nedes knowe your hevinesse;
I have pite to se you in ony distresse.
If ony have you wronged, ye shall revenged be
Thoughe I on the grounde be slaine for the[e],
220 Though that I knowe before that I sholde die!

Everyman. Verily, Felawship, gramercy.

Felawship. Tusshe! by thy thanks I set not a strawe.
Shewe me your grefe and saye no more.

Everyman. If I my herte sholde to you breke,
225 And then you to tourne your minde fro me
And wolde not me comforte whan ye here me speke,
Then sholde I ten times sorier be.

Felawship. Sir, I saye as I will do indede.

Everyman. Then be you a good frende at nede.
230 I have founde you true herebefore,

Felawship. And so ye shall evermore.
For, in faith, and thou go to Hell,
I will not forsake the[e] by the waye.

Everyman. Ye speke like a good frende; I bileve you well.
235 I shall deserve it and I may.

Felawship. I speke of no deservinge, by this daye!
For he that will saye and nothinge do
Is not worthy with good company to go.
Therfore shewe me the grefe of your minde
240 As to your frende moost lovinge and kinde.

Everyman. I shall shewe you how it is:
Commaunded I am to go a journaye,
A longe waye harde and daungerous,
And give a straite counte without delaye
245 Before the hie Juge, Adonai.
Wherfore, I pray you, bere me company,
As ye have promised, in this journaye.

Felawship. That is mater in dede! Promise is duty,

But, and I sholde take suche a vyage on me,
250   I knowe it well, it sholde be to my paine.
Also it make*th* me aferde, certaine.
But let us take counsell here as well as we can,
For your wordes wolde fere a stronge man.

Everyman. Why, ye said if I had nede
255   Ye wolde me never forsake, quicke ne deed,
Thoughe it were to Hell, truely.

Felawship. So I said, certainely,
But suche pleasures be set aside, the sothe to saye.
And also, if we toke suche a journaye,
260   Whan sholde we againe come?

Everyman. Naye, never againe till the daye of dome.

Felawship. In faith, then will not I come there!
Who hath you these tidinges brought?

Everyman. In dede, Deth was with me here.

265 *Felawship.* Now, by God that all hathe bought,
If Deth were the messenger,
For no man that is livinge to-daye
I will not go that lothe journaye——
Not for the fader that bigate me!

270 *Everyman.* Ye promised other wise, pardé.

Felawship. I wote well I said so, truely.
And yet, if thou wilte ete and drinke and make good chere,
Or haunt to women the lusty company,
I wolde not forsake you while the day is clere,
275   Trust me verily.

Everyman. Ye[a], therto ye wolde be redy!
To go to mirthe, solas, and playe
Your minde will soner apply
Than to bere me company in my long journaye.

280 *Felawship.* Now, in good faith, I will not that waye,
But, and thou will murder or ony man kill,

In that I will helpe the[e] with a good will.

Everyman. O, that is a simple advise indede!
Gentill felawe, helpe me in my necessite!
285   We have loved longe, and now I nede,
And now, gentill Felawship, remembre me.

Felawship. Wheder ye have loved me or no,
By Saint Johan, I will not with the[e] go!

Everyman. Yet, I pray the[e], take the labour and do so moche for me
290   To bringe me forwarde, for saint charite,
And comforte me till I come without the towne.

Felawship. Nay, and thou wolde give me a newe gowne,
I will not a fote with the[e] go,
But, and thou had taried, I wolde not have lefte the[e] so.
295   And as now God spede the[e] in thy journaye,
For from the[e] I will departe as fast as I maye.

Everyman. Wheder a way, Felawship? Will thou forsake me?

Felawship. Ye[a] by my faye! To God I betake the[e].

Everyman. Farewell, good Felawship! For the[e] my herte is sore.
300   Adewe for ever! I shall se the[e] no more.

Felawship. In faith, Everyman, fare well now at the end*inge*!
For you I will remembre that partinge is mourninge.

Everyman. Alacke, shall we th*u*s departe indede——
A, Lady, helpe!——without ony more comforte?
305   Lo, Felawship forsaketh me in my moost nede.
For helpe in this worlde wheder shall I resorte?
Felawship here-before with me wolde mery make,
And now litell sorowe for me dooth he take.
It is said, "In prosperite men frendes may finde,
310   Whiche in adversite be full unkinde."
Now wheder for socoure shall I flee
Sith that Felawship hath forsaken me?
To my kinnesmen I will, truely,
Prayenge them to helpe me in my necessite.
315   I bileve that they will do so,

For kinde will crepe where it may not go.
I will go 'saye, for yonder I se them...
Where be ye now, my frendes and kinnesmen?

Kinrede.   Here be we now at your commaundement.
320   Cosin, I praye you shewe us your entent
In ony wise and not spare.

Cosin.   Ye[a], Everyman, and to us declare
If ye be disposed to go ony-whider,
For, wete you well, *we* will live and die togider.

325 *Kinrede.* In welth and wo we will with you *h*olde,
For over his kinne a man may be *b*olde.

Everyman. Gramercy, my frendes and kinnesmen kinde.
Now shall I shewe you the grefe of my minde:
I was commaunded by a messenger,
330   That is a hie kinges chefe officer.
He bad me go a pilgrimage, to my paine,
And I knowe well I shall never come againe.
Also I must give a rekeninge straite,
For I have a great enemy that hath me in waite,
335   Which entendeth me for to hinder.

Kinrede.   What accounte is that whiche ye must render?
That wolde I knowe.

Everyman. Of all my workes I must shewe
How I have lived and my dayes spent:
340   Also of ill dedes that I have used
In my time, sith life was me lent,
And of all vertues that I have refused.
Therfore, I praye you, go thider with me
To helpe to make min accounte, for saint charite.

345 *Cosin.* What, to go thider? Is that the mater?
Nay, Everyman, I had lever fast brede and water
All this five yere and more.

Everyman. Alas, that ever I was bore!
For now shall I never be mery
350   If that you forsake me.

Kinrede.   A, sir, what ye be a mery man!
           Take good herte to you and make no mone.
           But one thinge I warne you, by Saint Anne:
           As for me, ye shall go alone.

355 *Everyman.* My Cosin, will you not with me go?

Cosin.   No, by our Lady! I have the crampe in my to[e].
           Trust not for me, for, so God me spede,
           I will deceive you in your moost nede.

Kinrede.   It availeth not us to 'tise.
360   Ye shall have my maide with all my herte;
           She loveth to go to feestes, there to be nise,
           And to daunce, and abrode to sterte.
           I will give her leve to helpe you in that journey
           If that you and she may agree.

365 *Everyman.* Now shewe me the very effecte of your minde:
           Will you go with me or abide behinde?

Kinrede.   Abide behinde? Ye[a], that will I and I maye!
           Therfore farewell till another daye.

Everyman. Howe sholde I be mery or gladde?
370   For faire promises men to me make,
           But whan I have moost nede they me forsake.
           I am deceived; that maketh me sadde.

Cosin.   Cosin Everyman, farewell now,
           For verily I will not go with you.
375   Also of mine owne an unredy rekeninge
           I have to accounte; therfore I make taryenge.
           Now God kepe the[e], for now I go.

Everyman. A, Jesus, is all come here-to?
           Lo, faire wordes maketh fooles faine;
380   They promise and nothinge will do, certaine.
           My kinnesmen promised me faithfully
           For to abyde with me stedfastly,
           And now fast awaye do they flee.
           Even so Felawship promised me.
385   What frende were best me of to provide?

I lose my time here longer to abide.
Yet in my minde a thinge there is:
All my life I have loved riches;
If that my Good now helpe me might,
390   He wolde make my herte full light.
I will speke to him in this distresse.
Where arte thou, my Gooddes and riches?

Goodes.   Who calleth me? Everyman? What, hast thou haste?
          I lie here in corners, trussed and piled so hie,
395   And in chestes I am locked so fast,
          Also sacked in bagges. Thou mayst se with thin[e] eye
          I cannot stire; in packes lowe I lie.
          What wolde ye have? Lightly me saye.

Everyman. Come hider, Good, in al the hast[e] thou may,
400   For of counseill I must desire the[e].

Goodes.   Sir, and ye in the worlde have sorowe or adversite,
          That can I helpe you to remedy shortly.

Everyman. It is another disease that greveth me;
          In this worlde it is not, I tell the[e] so.
405   I am sent for, another way to go,
          To give a straite counte generall
          Before the hiest Jupiter of all,
          And all my life I have had joye and pleasure in the[e];
          Therfore I pray the[e], go with me,
410   For, paraventure, thou mayst before God Almighty
          My rekeninge helpe to clene and purifye,
          For it is said ever amonge
          That "money maketh all right that is wronge."

Goodes.   Nay, Everyman, I singe another songe.
415   I folowe no man in suche vyages,
          For, and I wente with the[e],
          Thou sholdes*t* fare moche the worse for me.
          For bicause on me thou did set thy minde,
          Thy rekeninge I have made blotted and blinde,
420   That thine accounte thou cannot make truly——
          And that hast thou for the love of me!

Everyman. That wolde greve me full sore

Whan I sholde come to that ferefull answere.
Up, let us go thider togider.

425 *Goodes*. Nay, not so! I am to[o] britell; I may not endure.
I will folowe *no* man one fote, be ye sure.

Everyman. Alas, I have the[e] loved and had grete pleasure
All my life-dayes on good and treasure.

Goodes.   That is to thy dampnacion, without lesinge,
430   For my love is contrary to the love everlastinge.
           But, if thou had me loved moderately duringe,
           As to the poore give parte of me,
           Than sholdest thou not in this dolour be,
           Nor in this grete sorowe and care.

435 *Everyman*. Lo, now was I deceived or I was ware,
And all I may wite my spendinge of time.

Goodes.   What, wenest thou that I am thine?

Everyman. I had went so.

Goodes.   Naye, Everyman, I saye no.
440   As for a while I was lente the[e];
           A season thou hast had me in prosperite.
           My condicioun is mannes soule to kill;
           If I save one, a thousande I do spill.
           Wenest thou that I will folowe the[e]?
445   Nay, fro this worlde not, verile.

Everyman. I had wende otherwise.

Goodes.   Therfore to thy soule Good is a thefe,
           For whan thou arte deed, this is my gise:
           Another to deceive in this same wise
450   As I have done the[e], and all to his soules reprefe.

Everyman. O false Good, cursed thou be,
Thou traitour to God, that hast deceived me
And caught me in thy snare!

Goodes.   Mary, thou brought thy selfe in care,

455   Wherof I am gladde.
               I must nedes laugh; I cannot be sadde.

Everyman. A[h], Good, thou hast had longe my hertely love;
               I gave the[e] that whiche sholde be the Lordes above.
               But wilte thou not go with me indede?
460   I praye the[e] trouth to saye.

Goodes. No, so God me spede!
               Therfore farewell and have good daye.

Everyman. O, to whome shall I make my mone
               For to go with me in that hevy journaye?
465   First Felawship said he wolde with me gone.
               His wordes were very pleasaunt and gaye,
               But afterwarde he lefte me alone.
               Then spake I to my kinnesmen, all in dispaire.
               And also they gave me wordes faire;
470   They lacked no faire spekinge,
               But all forsoke me in the endinge.
               Then wente I to my Goodes that I loved best,
               In hope to have comforte, but there had I leest,
               For my Goodes sharply did me tell
475   That he bringeth many into Hell.
               Then of myselfe I was ashamed,
               And so I am worthy to be blamed;
               Thus may I well myselfe hate.
               Of whome shall I now counseill take?
480   I thinke that I shall never spede
               Till that I go to my Good Dede.
               But, alas, she is so weke
               That she can nother go nor speke;
               Yet will I venter on her now.
485   My Good Dedes, where be you?

Good Dedes. Here I lie, colde in the grounde.
               Thy sinnes hath me sore bounde,
               That I can not stere.

Everyman. O Good Dedes, I stande in fere!
490   I must you pray of counseill,
               For helpe now sholde come right well.

Good Dedes. Everyman, I have understandinge
        That ye be somoned acounte to make
        Before Myssias, of Jherusalem kinge;
495   And you do by me, that journay with you will I take.

Everyman. Therfore I come to you my moone to make.
        I praye you that ye will go with me.

Good Dedes. I wolde full faine, but I cannot stande, verily.

Everyman. Why, is there onythinge on you fall?

500 *Good Dedes*. Ye[a], sir, I may thanke you of all.
        If ye had parfitely chered me,
        Your boke of counte full redy had be.
        Loke, the bokes of your workes and dedes eke
        Ase how they lie under the fete,
505   To your soules hevines.

Everyman. Our Lorde Jesus helpe me!
        For one letter here I cannot se.

Good Dedes. There is a blinde rekeninge in time of distres!

Everyman. Good Dedes, I praye you helpe me in this nede,
510   Or elles I am for ever dampned indede;
        Therfore helpe me to make rekeninge
        Before the Redemer of all thinge,
        That Kinge is, and was, and ever shall.

Good Dedes. Everyman, I am sory of your fall,
515   And faine wolde I helpe you and I were able.

Everyman. Good Dedes, your counseill I pray you give me.

Good Dedes. That shall I do, verily.
        Thoughe that on my fete I may not go,
        I have a sister that shall with you also,
520   Called Knowlege, whiche shall with you abide,
        To helpe you to make that dredefull rekeninge.

Knowlege. Everyman, I will go with the[e] and be thy gide,
        In thy moost nede to go by thy side.

Everyman. In good condicion I am now in every thinge
525   And am [w]holy content with this good thinge,
    Thanked be God my Creature!

Good Dedes. And whan she hath brought you there
    Where thou shalte hele the[e] of thy smarte,
    Then go you with your rekeninge and your Good Dedes togider,
530   For to make you joyfull at herte
    Before the Blessyd Trinite.

Everyman. My Good Dedes, gramercy!
    I am well content, certainly,
    With your wordes swete.

535 *Knowlege*. Now go we togider lovingly
    To Confession, that clensinge rivere.

Everyman. For joy I wepe; I wolde we were there!
    But, I pray you, give me cognicion
    Where dwelleth that holy man Confession.

540 *Knowlege*. In the hous of salvacion;
    We shall finde him in that place
    That shall us comforte, by Goddes grace.
    Lo, this is Confession. Knele downe and aske mercy,
    For he is in good conceite with God Almighty.

545 *Everyman*. O glorious fountaine, that all unclennes doth clarify,
    Wasshe fro me the spottes of vice unclene,
    That on me no sinne may be sene.
    I come with Knowlege for my redempcion,
    Repent with herte and full contricion,
550   For I am commaunded a pilgrimage to take
    And grete accountes before God to make.
    Now I praye you, Shrifte, moder of salvacion,
    Helpe my Good Dedes for my piteous exclamacion.

Confession. I knowe your sorowe well, Everyman.
555   Bycause with Knowlege ye come to me,
    I will you comforte as well as I can.
    And a precious jewell I will give the[e],
    Called penaunce, . . .voider of adversite;
    Therwith shall your body chastised be

560   With abstinence and perseveraunce in Goddes service.
      Here shall you receive that scourge of me
      Which is penaunce stronge, that ye must endure
      To remembre thy Saviour was scourged for the[e]
      With sharpe scourges and suffred it paciently;
565   So must thou or thou scape that painful pilgrimage.
      Knowlege, kepe him in this vyage,
      And by that time Good Dedes will be with the[e].
      But in ony wise be seker of mercy,
      For your time draweth fast. And ye will saved be,
570   Aske God mercy, and he will graunte truely.
      Whan with the scourge of penaunce man doth him binde,
      The oile of forgivenes than shall he finde.

Everyman. Thanked be God for His gracious werke!
      For now I will my penaunce begin.
575   This hath rejoised and lighted my herte
      Though the knottes be painful and harde, within.

Knowlege. Everyman, loke your penaunce that ye fulfill
      What paine that ever it to you be,
      And Knowlege shall give you counseill at will
580   How your accounte ye shall make clerely.

Everyman. O eternall God, O hevenly figure,
      O way of rightwisness, O goodly vision,
      Which discended downe in a virgin pure
      Bycause he wolde every man redeme,
585   Whiche Adam forfaited by his disobedience.
      O blessid Godheed, electe and hie devine,
      Forgive *me* my grevous offence!
      Here I crye the[e] mercy in this presence.
      O ghostly treasure, O raunsomer and redemer,
590   Of all the worlde hope and conduiter,
      Mirrour of joye, foundatour of mercy,
      Whiche enlumineth Heven and erth therby,
      Here my clamorous complaint though it late be.
      Receive my prayers, unworthy in this hevy life!
595   Though I be a sinner moost abhominable,
      Yet let my name be writen in Moyses table.
      O Mary, praye to the Maker of all thinge,
      Me for to helpe at my endinge,
      And save me fro the power of my enemy,

600   For Deth assaileth me strongly.
        And, Lady, that I may by meane of thy prayer
        Of your Sones glory to be partinere,
        By the meanes of His passion, I it crave.
        I beseche you helpe my soule to save!
605   Knowlege, give me the scourge of penaunce;
        My flesshe therwith shall give acqueintaunce.
        I will now begin if God give me grace.

Knowlege. Everyman, God give you time and space!
        Thus I bequeth you in the handes of our Saviour.
610   Now may you make your rekeninge sure.

Everyman. In the name of the Holy Trinite,
        My body sore punisshed shall be.
        Take this, body, for the sinne of the flesshe!
        Also thou delitest to go gay and fresshe,
615   And in the way of dampnacion thou did me bringe;
        Therfore suffre now strokes of punisshinge.
        Now of penaunce I will wade the water clere
        To save me from Purgatory, that sharpe fire.

Good Dedes. I thanke God, now I can walke and go,
620   And am delivered of my sikenesse and wo.
        Therfore with Everyman I will go and not spare;
        His good workes I will helpe him to declare.

Knowlege. Now, Everyman, be mery and glad!
        Your Good Dedes cometh now; ye may not be sad.
625   Now is your Good Dedes [w]hole and sounde,
        Goinge upright upon the grounde.

Everyman. My herte is light, and shal be evermore;
        Now will I smite faster than I dide before.

Good Dedes. Everyman, pilgrime, my speciall frende,
630   Blessyd be thou without ende!
        For the[e] is preparate the eternall glory.
        Ye have me made [w]hole and sounde;
        Therfore I will bide by the[e] in every stounde.

Everyman. Welcome, my Good Dedes! Now I here thy voice
635   I wepe for very swetenes of love.

Knowlege. Be no more sad, but ever rejoice;
           God seeth thy livinge in His trone above.
           Put on this garment to thy behove,
           Whiche is wette with your teres,
640   Or elles before God you may it misse,
           Whan ye to your journeys ende come shall.

Everyman. Gentill Knowlege, what do ye it call?

Knowlege. It is a garment of sorowe;
           Fro paine it will you borowe.
645   Contricion it is
           That getteth forgivenes;
           He pleaseth God passinge well.

Good Dedes. Everyman, will you were it for your hele?

Everyman. Now blessyd be Jesu, Maryes sone,
650   For now have I on true contricion,
           And lette us go now without taryenge.
           Good Dedes, have we clere our rekeninge?

Good Dedes. Ye[a], in dede, I have *it* here.

Everyman. Then I trust we nede not fere.
655   Now, frendes, let us not parte in twaine.

Knowlege. Nay, Everyman, that will we not, certaine.

Good Dedes. Yet must thou lede with the[e]
           Thre persones of grete might.

Everyman. Who sholde they be?

660 *Good Dedes.* Discrecion and Strength they hight,
           And thy Beaute may not abide behinde.

Knowlege. Also ye must call to minde
           Your Five Wittes as for your counseilours.

Good Dedes. You must have them redy at all houres.

665 *Everyman.* Howe shall I gette them hider?

Knowlege. You must call them all togider,
And they will here you incontinent.

Everyman. My frendes, come hider and be present,
Discrecion, Strengthe, my Five Wittes, and Beaute.

670 *Beaute.* Here at your will we be all redy.
What *wolde* ye that we sholde do?

Good Dedes. That ye wolde with Everyman go
And helpe him in his pilgrimage.
Advise you, will ye with him or not in that vyage?

675 *Strength.* We will bringe him all thider,
To his helpe and comforte, ye may beleve me.

Discrecion. So will we go with him all togider.

Everyman. Almighty God, loved *may* Thou be!
I give The[e] laude that I have hider brought
680   Strength, Discrecion, Beaute, and V. Wittes. Lacke I nought.
And my Good Dedes, with Knowlege clere,
All be in company at my will here.
I desire no more to my besines.

Strengthe. And I, Strength, will by you stande in distres,
685   Though thou wolde in bataile fight on the grounde.

V. Wittes. And though it were thrugh the worlde rounde,
We will not departe for swete ne soure.

Beaute. Nor more will I unto dethes houre,
Whatsoever therof befall.

690 *Discrecion.* Everyman, advise you first of all;
Go with a good advisement and deliberacion.
We all give you vertuous monicion
That all shall be well.

Everyman. My frendes, harken what I will tell——
695   I praye God rewarde you in His hevenly sp[h]ere——
Now herken, all that be here,
For I will make my testament

Here before you all present:
In almes halfe my good I will give with my handes twaine
700 In the way of charite, with good entent,
And the other halfe still shall remaine
In queth, to be retourned there it ought to be.
This I do in despite of the Fende of Hell,
To go quite out of his perell
705 Ever after and this daye.

Knowlege. Everyman, herken what I saye:
Go to Presthode, I you advise,
And receive of him in ony wise
The Holy Sacrament and Ointement togider.
710 Than shortly se ye tourne againe hider;
We will all abide you here.

V. Wittes. Ye[a], Everyman, hie you that ye redy were.
There is no emperour, kinge, duke, ne baron
That of God hath commicion
715 As hath the leest preest in the worlde beinge,
For of the blessyd sacramentes pure and benigne
He bereth the keyes, and therof hath the cure
For mannes redempcion——it is ever sure——
Whiche God for our soules medicine
720 Gave us out of His herte with grete pine.
Here in this transitory life, for the[e] and me,
The blessyd sacramentes vii. there be:
Baptim, Confirmacion, with Preesthode good,
And the Sacrament of Goddes precious Flesshe and Blod,
725 Mariage, the holy Extreme Unccion, and Penaunce.
These seven be good to have in remembraunce,
Gracious sacramentes of hie devinite.

Everyman. Faine wolde I receive that Holy Body,
And mekely to my ghostly fader I will go.

730 *V. Wittes.* Everyman, that is the best that ye can do.
God will you to salvacion bringe,
For preesthode excedeth all other thinge.
To us Holy Scripture they do teche
And converteth man fro sinne, Heven to reche;
735 God hath to them more power given
Than to ony aungell that is in Heven.

<pre>
        With v. wordes he may consecrate
        Goddes body in flesshe and blode to make,
        And handeleth his Maker bitwene his handes.
740   The preest bindeth and unbindeth all bandes,
        Bothe in erthe and in Heven.
        Thou ministres all the sacramentes seven;
        Though we kisse thy fete, thou were worthy.
        Thou arte surgyon that cureth sinne deedly;
745   No remedy we finde under God
        But all onely preesthode.
        Everyman, God gave preest that dignite
        And setteth them in his stede amonge us to be;
        Thus be they above aungelles in degree.

750 Knowlege. If preestes be good, it is so, suerly.
        But whan Jesu hanged on the Crosse with grete smarte,
        There he gave out of His blessyd herte
        The seven sacramentes in grete tourment;
        He solde them not to us, that Lorde omnipotent.
755   Therfore Saint Peter the Apostell dothe saye
        That Jesus curse hath all they
        Whiche God their Saviour do b[u]y or sell,
        Or they for ony money do take or tell.
        Sinfull preestes giveth the sinners example bad:
760   Their children sitteth by other mennes fires, I have harde;
        And some haunteth womens company
        With unclene life, as lustes of lechery.
        These be with sinne made blinde.

V. Wittes. I trust to God no suche may we finde;
765   Therfore let us preesthode honour
        And folowe their doctrine for our soules socoure.
        We be their shepe, and they shepeherdes be,
        By whome we all be kepte in suerte.
        Peas, for yonder I se Everyman come,
770   Whiche hath made true satisfaccion.

Good Dedes. Me thinke it is he in dede.

Everyman. Now Jesu be your alder spede!
        I have received the Sacrament for my redempcion
        And then mine Extreme Unccion.
775   Blessyd be all they that counseiled me to take it!
</pre>

And now, frendes, let us go without longer respite.
I thanke God that ye have taried so longe.
Now set eche of you on this rodde your honde
And shortely folowe me.
780   I go before there I wolde be. God be *our* gide!

Strength.   Everyman, we will not fro you go
Till ye have done this vyage longe.

Discrecion.   I, Discrecion, will bide by you also.

Knowlege.   And though this pilgrimage be never so stronge,
785   I will never parte you fro.

Strength.   Everyman, I will be as sure by the[e]
As ever I dide by Judas Machabee.

Everyman.   Alas, I am so faint I may not stande;
My limmes under me *do* folde.
790   Frendes, let us not tourne againe to this lande,
Not for all the worldes golde,
For into this cave must I crepe
And tourne to erth, and there to slepe.

Beaute.   What, into this grave? Alas!

795 *Everyman.* Ye[a], there shall ye consume, more and lesse.

Beaute.   And what, sholde I smoder here?

Everyman.   Ye[a], by my faith, and never more appere.
In this worlde live no more we shall,
But in Heven before the hiest Lorde of all.

800 *Beaute.* I crosse out all this! Adewe, by Saint Johan!
I take my tappe in my lappe and am gone.

Everyman.   What, Beaute, whider will ye?

Beaute.   Peas! I am defe. I loke not behinde me,
Not and thou *wolde* give me all the golde in thy chest.

805 *Everyman.* Alas, wherto may I truste?

Beaute gothe fast awaye fro me.
She promised with me to live and die.

Strength.   Everyman, I will the[e] also forsake and denye;
Thy game liketh me not at all.

810 *Everyman.* Why, then, ye will forsake me all?
Swete Strength, tary a litell space.

Strength.   Nay, sir, by the rode of grace!
I will hie me from the[e] fast
Though thou wepe to thy herte tobrast.

815 *Everyman.* Ye wolde ever bide by me, ye said.

Strength.   Ye[a], I have you ferre inoughe conveyde.
Ye be olde inoughe, I understande,
Your pilgrimage to take on hande.
I repent me that I hider came.

820 *Everyman.* Strength, you to displease I am to blame.
Will ye breke promise that is dette?

Strength.   In faith, I care not.
Thou arte but a foole to complaine;
You spende your speche and wast[e] your braine.
825   Go thrist the[e] into the grounde!

Everyman. I had wende surer I sholde you have founde.
He that trusteth in his Strength,
She him deceiveth at the length.
Bothe Strength and Beaute forsaketh me;
830   Yet they promised me faire and lovingly.

Discrecion. Everyman, I will after Strength be gone.
As for me, I will leve you alone.

Everyman. Why, Discrecion, will ye forsake me?

Discrecion. Ye[a] in faith, I will go fro the[e],
835   For whan Strength goth before
I folowe after evermore.

Everyman. Yet, I pray the[e], for the love of the Trinite,
         Loke in my grave ones piteously.

Discrecion. Nay, so nie will I not come.
840   Farewell, everichone!

Everyman. O, all thinge faileth save God alone——
         Beaute, Strength, and Discrecion,
         For whan Deth bloweth his blast,
         They all renne fro me full fast.

845 *V. Wittes*. Everyman, my leve now of the[e] I take.
         I will folowe the other, for here I the[e] forsake.

Everyman. Alas, then may I waile and wepe,
         For I toke you for my best frende.

V. Wittes. I will no lenger the[e] kepe.
850   Now farewell, and there an ende.

Everyman. O Jesu, helpe! All hath forsaken me.

Good Dedes. Nay, Everyman, I will bide with the[e].
         I will not forsake the[e] indede;
         Thou shalte finde me a good frende at nede.

855 *Everyman*. Gramercy, Good Dedes! Now may I true frendes se.
         They have forsaken me, everichone;
         I loved them better than my Good Dedes alone.
         Knowlege, will ye forsake me also?

Knowlege. Ye[a], Everyman, whan ye to Deth shall go,
860   But not yet, for no maner of daunger.

Everyman. Gramercy, Knowlege, with all my herte.

Knowlege. Nay, yet I will not from hens departe
         Till I se where ye shall become.

Everyman. Me thinke, alas, that I must be gone
865   To make my rekeninge and my dettes paye,
         For I se my time is nie spent awaye.
         Take example, all ye that this do here or se.

How they that I loved best do forsake me
Excepte my Good Dedes that bideth truely.

870 *Good Dedes*. All erthly thinges is but vanite:
Beaute, Strength, and Discrecion do man forsake,
Folisshe frendes and kinnesmen that faire spake——
All fleeth save Good Dedes, and that am I.

Everyman. Have mercy on me, God moost mighty,
875   And stande by me, thou moder and maide, Holy Mary!

Good Dedes. Fere not; I will speke for the[e].

Everyman. Here I crye God mercy.

Good Dedes. Shorte our ende and minisshe our paine;
Let us go and never come againe.

880 *Everyman*. Into Thy handes, Lorde, my soule I commende;
Receive it, Lorde, that it be not lost.
As Thou me boughtest, so me defende,
And save me from the Fendes boost
That I may appere with that blessyd hoost
885   That shall be saved at the day of dome.
In manus tuas, of mightes moost
For ever, *Commendo spiritum meum*.

Knowlege. Now hath he suffred that we all shall endure;
The Good Dedes shall make all sure.
890   Now hath he made endinge.
Me thinketh that I here aungelles singe
And make grete joy and melody
Where Everymannes soule received shall be.

The Aungell. Come, excellente electe spouse, to Jesu!
895   Here above thou shalte go
Bycause of thy singuler vertue.
Now thy soule is taken thy body fro,
Thy rekeninge is crystall-clere.
Now shalte thou into the hevenly sp[h]ere,
900   Unto the whiche all ye shall come
That liveth well before the daye of dome.

Doctour.   This morall men may have in minde.
          Ye herers, take it of worth, olde and yonge,
          And forsake Pride, for he deceiveth you in the ende.
905   And remembre Beaute, V. Wittes, Strength, and Discrecion,
          They all at the last do Everyman forsake
          Save his Good Dedes there dothe he take.
          But beware, *for* and they be small,
          Before God he hath no helpe at all.
910   None excuse may be there for Everyman.
          Alas, how shall he do then?
          For after dethe amendes may no man make,
          For then mercy and pite doth him forsake.
          If his rekeninge be not clere whan he doth come,
915   God will saye, "*Ite, maledicti, in ignem eternum.*"
          And he that hath his accounte [w]hole and sounde,
          Hie in Heven he shall be crounde.
          Unto whiche place God bringe us all thider,
          That we may live body and soule togider.
920   Therto helpe the Trinite!
          Amen, saye ye, for saint charite.

FINIS
Thus endeth this morall playe of Everyman.
Imprinted at London in Poules
chyrche yarde by me
Johan Skot.

NOTES ON THE TRANSLATION OF *ELCKERLIJC*

13-14. As already indicated, these lines are troublesome. *Mits* is not a conjunction but a preposition, and as a preposition governs only the third or fourth case (see *Mnl. W.* IV, 1566); *mits dat* is indeed a conjunction, however (see 1569). Literally "des" translates as "for which."

18. *have*: literally "has."

22. *they*: literally "it."

38. *for naught*: literally "lost."

39. *at such a price*: literally "so costly."

48. *at any time*: literally "at all hours."

78. *As I shall make clear to you*: literally "As I to you shall lay before [your] eyes." Cf. 202.

97. *Plainly* ("bloot"): a filler for the sake of rime (cf. Vos).

107. *in this regard*: literally "with regard to this."

120. *I see no way out*: literally "I do not see how to put sleeves to it."

131. . . . "it is that" has been omitted.

146. *So*: literally "that."

175. *'tis*: the contraction is in the original (cf. 348, 529, 787, 807, 876; the instance in 265 of the translation originates there, however). This colloquial construction is in keeping with the relative simplicity of the style of *Elckerlijc*. Its author has even been described as "taalpover" by Willem Asselbergs in *De Stijl van Elkerlijk* (Zwolle, 1968), p. 33.

196. Or, freely, "You are just a bundle of distress."

204. The redundant "daer" ("then") has been omitted.

207. *immeasurably* (*boven screve*): literally "beyond the boundary line."

208. *I have never found* etc.: literally "I have never found something else in you but loyalty."

216. *would not prove it in deeds*: literally "did not let it appear in deeds."

228. *binding*: "van waerden" means literally "in force," a juridical phrase (cf. *Mnl. W.*, IX, 2164-65, under *werde*, 2; also *O. E. D.* under *force*, 8c); modern Dutch: "van kracht."

238. *to put it bluntly*: more literally "frankly and straightforward."

259. *it*: on the assumption that "wilt" is a contraction of *wilt+het→wilt−et→wilt.*

264. *Such harping on loyalty*: literally "Loyalty here, loyalty there!" With acknowledgment to Prof. Jarrott for the adopted paraphrase, which follows W.H. Beuken's edition of *Elckerlijc*. On the preceding locution, cf. "'Canada here, Canada there,' she replied testily," *Cousin Phillis*, in *Cousin Phillis and Other Tales by Mrs. Gaskell* (London, 1906), p. 88.

265. *that's that*: literally "there-with closed." Cf. 783.

290. *that I may live*: "opdat ic leve" may also be construed as conditional, "if I [have time to] live."

315. *Is not something* etc.: literally "Is it wanting not more?"

317. *I am knocked over*: literally "I fall on my buttocks."

351. *useless*: literally "lost." Cf. 795 and 807.

367. *If something*: "You have" has been omitted.

429. *reckoned*: after Vos even though *to reckon* is not given as a meaning of *passen* in *Mnl. W.*

439. *has been damned*: literally "is in damnation."

454. *you have made me*: after Vos and Steenbergen; cf. *Mnl. W.*, IX, 715, under *voegen*, I, B 1.

459. *about that I should like to complain. . .*: literally "that will be complained. . ."

474. *with a sincere heart*: after Vos; cf. *Mnl. W.*, II, 2173-74, under *gront*, 4.

491. *God must be praised* etc.: literally "God's praise must therein be honored."

555. *of eminent worth*: literally "out-chosen." Cf. 886.

591. *wherever you might*: or "were [it] so that you might."

651. here: literally "there".

659. [listen to]: cf. *Elck.* 675.

729. *And make heaps of money out of it*: literally "And there-of make money with heaps."

733. *of living*: or perhaps "of body."

735. *does*: on the assumption that "doet" refers to "sitten" (732) rather than to "zijn" (734).

740. *Let this be sufficient warning*: literally "Let this no longer be warning."

758. *has to*: literally "will have to."

767-68. *Yes, such stuff/ We must become*: literally "Yes, of this worth/ So we must become."

772. *I take back* etc.: literally "score my scot" (the *O. E. D.*, under *score*, v., II, 7, does not document the meaning *cancel* until the late seventeenth century, however).

781. *not altogether*: literally "not as it should be." An understatement.

784. *please*: literally "(wait) still!"

786. *Ende*: H; L, B *En*; M *Ay* (after Van Elslander, who cites J.W. Muller). "En" is a negative adverb, scarcely in keeping with Cracht's reply, "Ja, ic. . ." ("Will you *not* leave me then?"/ "Yes. . .").

798. *He*: literally "she" (grammatical gender).

816. *leave*: literally "away."

835. *pay my debt* (cf. 857): that is, the debt of nature; cf. Vos's note and *O. E. D.*, under *debt*, 4b. Cooper and Wortham unfortunately accept E.R. Tigg's translation of "gelden," namely, "to suffer for the sins of others" (*JEGP*, 38 [1939], 584), construing it as support for the notion, associated with T.F. van Laan and R.A. Potter, that "Everyman has become a Christ figure by this time" (note on line 888 of C & W).

876. *bear this in mind*: literally "be of this to inwards." Under *binnen*, II, 4, a, the *Mnl. W.*, I, 1266, glosses "te binnen sijn" as "to be well informed about."

882. *perish*: hypothetical (see corresponding note on *gadi*, Notes on the Text of *Elckerlijc*).

NOTES ON THE TEXT OF *ELCKERLIJC*

The early copies of *Elckerlijc* are abbreviated as follows: Vorsterman print, Leiden University Library, L; print in the Royal Library, Brussels, B; print in the Royal Library, The Hague, H; manuscript, Royal Library, Brussels, M.

The editions of *Elckerlijc* cited are designated only by the last name of the editor and are identified in the preface (see note 23) except for Logeman, which refers to *Elckerlijk... and Everyman*, ed. Henri Logeman (Ghent, 1892). The *Middelnederlandsch Woordenboek*, ed. E. Verwijs and J. Verdam ('s-Gravenhage, 1885-1952), 11 vols., appears as *Mnl. W.*, the pages of which are numbered by columns.

In the accompanying text, which usually follows the lineation of Vos's edition, the extra line in group numbered 595-600 of his edition has been eliminated by reducing "Dies wil ic bi hem gaen te tijde" (Vos) to a half line, as in *Den Spyeghel der Salicheyt van Elckerlijc*, ed. K.H. de Raaf (Groningen, 1897), p. 58, line 581. In groups 250-55 and 795-800 Van Elslander's lineation has been followed.

Spyeghel: that is, in general a reflection of reality or truth. In the Middle Ages and Renaissance a common term for a compendium, sometimes admonitory, as in the epilogue of *Elckerlijc* (887-89): "Merct desen spieghel, hebten voer oghen..." In *Everyman mirror* appears only in the sense of *exemplar*, in an improvised phrase applied to God, "Myrrour of ioye" (591), but "treatyse" following the title may be intended as a translation of "spyeghel." On the metaphor of the mirror, see Herbert Grabes, *The Mutable Glass, Mirror Imagery in Titles and Texts of the Middle Ages and the English Renaissance*, trans. from the German by Gordon Collier (Cambridge, England, and New York, 1983). The original title less subtitle is *Speculum, Mirror, and Looking Glass* (Tübingen, 1973).

Elckerlijc: Literally *each* (*-lijc*) *of all* (*elcker-*); cf. *Mnl. W.* II, 614, under *elkerlijc*. On the use of this word as a pronominal adjective, cf. "elckerlijc mensche," title page and incipit.

esbamente: ordinarily means a diverting play or farce (see *Een Esbattement van sMenschen Sin en Verganckelijcke Schoonheit* [Zwolle, 1967], p. 107). Editors of *Elckerlijc* have defined this example of the term as a "stage play" (Steenbergen), a "short stage play" (Vos), and even as a "closet drama" (Endepols). The definition kindly supplied by Prof. Hummelen is preferable: "within this context a *short* play with *few* characters."

3. *uut vresen*: "without fear" of Me, that is (after Vos).

3. *onbekent*: a crux. The literal meaning is *ignorant*; other meanings are *dwaas* (*foolish*), *verblind* (*blinded*), and *verhard* (*hardened* or *hardhearted*); cf. Van Mierlo, p. 42, and *Mnl. W.*, V, 232-34, under *onbekent*, B. The ignorance, it should be stressed,

is willful; the collocation "uut vresen, onbekent" suggests not only folly but also hardening of the heart.

4. *Oec*: a crux. The meaning may be purely argumentative, or *likewise* or *nay*, *even*, or perhaps expressive of a causal relation with the preceding; *also* in the sense of *further* seems most likely.

10. Deletion: *die*, carried over from − *die* in preceding word; lacking in B, H, M.

12. *ghetoghen*; B, H: M *getoghen*; L *ghetoghe* (*the act of showing, description, apparition*).

13. *den*: editorial (L, B, H *der*; M *de*). The emendation is required if ".vij. dootsonden" be the indirect object of "Es op ghedaen."

13-14. Some editors, resorting to M, supply as subject "myn wrake," i.e., "By the Seven Deadly Sins my vengeance has been unleashed."

30. *Mijn. . .ghelove*: a crux. Vos, who does not offer a grammatical precedent, paraphrases as "belief. . .in Me," whereas Van Mierlo argues that an "objective" belief is meant, i.e. "the content" itself as distinct from the believer (pp. 44-45).

31. *selve*: B; L, H *selven* (*selves*).

32. *cranct*: B, H, M; L *branct* (printing error).

42. *hem recht toe hoort*: a crux in relation to "ic hem vry heb verleent" (40). The contradiction is not removed by Vos's appeal to the obligation of a medieval lord to guarantee his vassal the tenure of a fief. There is no reason to suspect corruption here.

45. *Elckerlijc*: L *elcktrlijc*.

88. *oversietse*: H; B *onersietse*; L *onersietste*; M *besietse*.

104. *mi*: B, H; M *my*; L *wi*.

107. *mi een*: B, H; M *my een*; L lacking.

107. *verdrach*: though it has been interpreted, with support from *Mnl. W.*, VIII, 1634 under *verdrach*, I, 1, as *exemption, remission* (cf. Vos and Steenbergen), in the context, both of the play and of medieval treatments of Death's summons, this interpretation seems very unlikely. In other occurrences of *verdrach* in *Elck. respite* seems to be meant (81, 185, as well as "verdraghet," 152); the instance in 115 − "uutstel noch verdrach" − is ambiguous.

111. *ghebieden*: B; H, M *gebieden*; L *ghedien* (*prosper, flourish*: dubious sense).

112. *verleeden*: pointing out the faulty rime (see *ghebieden*), Vos suggests that *vermieden* (*buy off*) may be the correct reading. Except for spelling there is no variant reading in this instance.

127. *bid. . .u*: B, H; M *biddick u*; L lacking.

148. *binnen*: M; L, H, *sinnen*; B gap in text. Evidently "sinnen" is due to eye-skip (see preceding line); Logeman notes (p. 15) that the word has been "crossed out in H"; cf. Vos.

179. *trecken* (all witnesses): Van Elslander, Steenbergen, and Van Mierlo (see his comment on p. 56) emend to *gane* for the sake of rime, but the unanimity of the witnesses suggests that this obvious emendation should be resisted.

183. *betrou*: B, H; M *betrouwe*; L *betron* (printing error).

191. *uwen noot*: M; B *uwen moet*; H *minen moet*; L *mijnen moet*. The reading "mijnen"seems senseless here; "noot" supplies a true rime, and Van Mierlo notes that in *Elckerlijc* "long *oo* everywhere regularly rimes with long *oo*, and *oe* with *oe*" (p. 17). Most recent editors favor "noot." including Vos, though he prints "moet."

194. *Want*: editorial (L, H, M *wat*; B gap in text).

199. *claer*: H, M; L lacking; B gap in text.

206. *meynet*: M *meent*; L *meyne*; H *meine*; B gap in text. The *t* (*it*) is enclitic.

213. *goet*: H, M; L lacking; B gap in text.

231. *desen*: B, H, M; L *deser* (probably a printing error since "gheruchte" is neuter and *van* usually governs the dative).

231. *gheruchte*: Vos takes this to mean *rumor* or *report*, but since Gheselscap did hear it, the conditional "soude" is nonsense. Thus Van Elslander's gloss is apparently correct: "last," or *misery* (cf. *Mnl. W.*, II, 1566, under *geruchte*, 4: "moeite, onaange- name toestand, verdriet, pijn").

243. *cracht*: B, H, M; L *crachte* (perhaps due to eye-skip; see "bode," 244).

259. *al*: B, H. M; L lacking.

284. *Vrient ende Maghe*: relatives on mother's side and relatives on father's side respectively; see Vos.

289. *niet*: B; H *nyet*; L *nient*; M line missing.

289. The *wel* in this example of the proverb is intrusive and does not appear in B (the line is missing in M). Cf. *Nederlandse spreekwoorden/spreuken en zegswijzen*, ed. K. ter Laan with A.M. Heidt Jr., 5th ed. (The Hague, 1967), p. 43, and *Deutsches Sprichwör- ter-Lexikon*, ed. Karl F.W. Wander (Darmstadt, 1964), I, 410. In the English versions *kind* or *kindness* is usually substituted for *blood* (cf. *Everyman*, 316, which does not repro- duce "wel," and *The James Carmichaell Collection of Proverbs in Scots*, ed. M.L. Ander- son [Edinburgh, 1957], p. 87, as well as B.J. Whiting, *Proverbs, Sentences, and Proverbial Phrases* [Cambridge, Mass., 1968], K34).

297. *Want*: B; L, H *wat*; M lacking.

323. *best* (also B, H): a *lectio difficilior* (M reads *beste*, n., i.e., *dear one* or *dear fellow*, which is followed by Van Elslander, Steenbergen, Van Mierlo, and Vos). Cf. *Mnl. W.*, I, 1092, under *best*, III, 4: "Laet ons best vlien," where "best" is clearly adverbial and has the meaning of *as fast as possible* ("Het spoedigst, zoo spoedig mogelijk").

328. *tot open tijde*: a juridical expression for the period when a lawsuit can be tried (see Vos and *Mnl. W.*, V, 1707, under *open*, 7). But the intended meaning is "until an indefinite time."

341. *doghen*: B, H; L *daghen* (misprint); M *dangier*.

388. *Want*: B, H, M; L *Wan*.

396. *oeck*: clearly adversative here; see *Mnl. W.* under *ooc*, 4.

396. *ghemint* (see Endepols): M *gemint*; L, B, H lacking.

407. *Hy proeft*: M; B *proeft*; L, H lacking.

427. *claghen*: only in L. Cf. *Everyman*, 463: "O, to whome shall I make my mone. . .?" The other witnesses read *ghewaghen* (M *gewaghen*), i.e. *mention*. According to Van Mierlo "claghen," which he regards as a corruption of the original reading, is important evidence that *Everyman* was translated from the Vorsterman print (pp. 22-5). Vos, without mentioning Van Mierlo, argues in his note, "It is not impossible that in the original text both words [i.e. "claghen"· and "ghewagen"] were present." He then cites two examples of such a collocation.

453. *Kan*: B, H; M *can*; L *han*.

456. *icx*: that is, *ik des* (cf. Endepols' note).

486. *heetse*: B, H (M *heetsse*); L *heeftse* (induced by *heb ic* in 485?).

492. *gheleyt*: editorial (B, M geleyt: L gheseyt [H gheseit] – nonsense).

497. *Elckerlijc*: H (B *Elckerlijck*; M *Elckerlyck*); L *Gheselscap*.

503. *Waer*: B, H, M; L *Wter* (printing error).

503. *Salicheden*: the suffix *en* need not be plural here.

509. *bloome*: all witnesses (with spelling variants). Though he retains this reading, Vos argues that it is a corruption of "borne" and that "the reading of *Everyman* is correct", i.e. "fountayne", 545. "Bloome" is defended by Van Mierlo (p. 78), who notes that *Homulus* renders the word as "o lilium. . .o floscule." "That the English has *fountayne* here," he concludes. "is but natural."

513. *behouwen*: B; L, H *behouwe*; M *berouwen*. Endepols prints *behouwe*, but the noun *behouw* (dat. *behouwe*) does not exist.

514. *versaecht*: B, H, M; L *versacht*.

516. *is*: B, H; L *es*; M *sy*.

517. *alst*: B; L, H, M *die*, apparently due to eye-skip (see preceding line).

520. *brieven*: M; B, H *brieve*; L *brienen* (printing error).

520. *Duecht*: H (B *doecht*, M *deucht*); L *ducht*.

528. *puere*: sense has apparently been sacrificed to rime; "puere" may be intended to suggest *purifying*.

558. *Saet*: L, B, H *scat* (M *schat*), or *treasure, hoard*. A crux. The emendation, which is adopted by Van Mierlo and Van Elslander, removes a false rime and redundancy, though both defects are to be found in *Elckerlijc* apart from a crux. Vos retains "scat" but in support of "saet" cites Rom. 1.3.

562. *beslaet*: H; B *doerslaet*, M *doorgaet*; L *bestaet* (a printing error).

566. *blade*: B, M; L, H *blader* (does not rime).

568. *almachtich*: B, H, M; L *almactich*.

574. *onrachtich*: B; L, H, M *onrastich* (*restless, unquiet*).

584. *Elckerlijc*: B, H (M *Elckerlyck*); L *Gheselscap*.

587. *so coen*: editorial. L, H *scoon* (B *scoen*, M *schoon*), or *beautiful, handsome*, makes little sense and a false rime. Vos notes that the reading "is usually emended" as given. *So* is presumably necessary to prepare the infinitive ("bringhen").

591 − 93: corrupt in all four witnesses (cf. Vos). In M 951 − 52 appear as one long variant: "Ay broeders, doet alle penitentie strange ende vruchtbarich. . ."

592. *waen*: apparently a variant of *waden* through syncope; see *Mnl. W.*, VI, 243, under *penitencie*, line 10.

593. *pelgrimaige*: M; L, B, H *penitencie*.

606. *sone der victorien*: B *here uutvercoren* (*lord elect*); M *sone geboren*.

617. *onghemoeyt*: H; B *oughemoeyt*, M *ongemoeyt*; L *onghemoet* (*dejected*).

621. *aendraghen*: H; B *aendragen*, M *aen. . .draghen*; L *aendragken* (printing error).

643. *Want* etc: B; M *om dat hy gedaecht is ter rekeninghen*; L, H lacking.

647. *Vroetscap*: equated with *wisdom* ("Wijsheyt," 631, 638), that is, practical wisdom or prudence, the directive virtue among the cardinal virtues (cf. St. Thomas Aquinas, *S. T.*, 1a 2ae, q. 60, a. 1). As he emphasizes (ibid., 2a 2ae, q. 47, a. 6), "The office of

prudence. . . is not to furnish ends for the moral virtues, but to settle means for attaining them" (trans. by Thomas Gilby, O.P., "Blackfriars" ed., *Summa Theologia*, 36 [New York and London, 1974], 23; the original reads "finem" rather than "fines," however). On prudence Josef Pieper observes, "To the contemporary mind, prudence seems less a prerequisite to goodness than an evasion of it," *Prudence*, trans. by Richard and Clara Winston (New York, 1959), p. 14. He also observes, "modern religious teachings have little or nothing to say about the place of prudence in life or in the hierarchy of virtues. Even the modern theologian who claims, or aspires, to be a follower of classical theology, displays the same uneasiness about prudence" (p. 17). In *Homulus* Vroetscap appears as Prudentia, one of three "formosae puellae" according to the cast of characters (as edited by Alphonse Roersch [Ghent, 1903], p. 3).

649. *Vroescap, Scoonheyt. . .ende Cracht*: Vos has noted that in Jewish literature, prudence, beauty, and strength are related to justice, "Over de betekenis van enkele allegorische figuren in de *Elckerlijc*," *Spiegel der Letteren*, 9 (1965), 26-27. In line 813 the triad are duly specified in climactic order: "Schoonheyt, Cracht, ende Vroescap groot."

653. *stout*: B, H, M; L *stont*.

668. *oetmoede*: B, H; L *oetmoet* (emended for sake of rime); M *oetmoedt*.

674. *desen*: B, H, M; L lacking.

678. *Tsacrament ende olijs* (cf. 745-46): Holy Communion and Extreme Unction.

683. *gave*: B, H, M; L *grave* (eye-skip).

691. *Sacramenten seven*: Biechte (Penance) is missing except in M, where it has been tacked on after "theylich olyzel" (Extreme Unction). In their edition of *Everyman*, cited in the preface, Cooper and Wortham argue (p. xxv), "It is probable that the omission from the Dutch text was deliberate and that it was the consequence of a controversy within the *Devotio Moderna*: from Groote onwards there had been some doubt about the value of sacramental absolution given by a priest in confession, on the ground that God alone converts the sinner. . ." On the contrary, the omission may well have been accidental, originating in a print shop, as the restoration in M suggests; if deliberate, the omission can scarcely be the author's, who let "Sacramenten seven" stand, and certainly there is no warrant for asserting that the "specific inclusion of the sacrament of penance in *Everyman* suggests the hand of a translator who was more conservative than his original author." Professor Wortham expands on the alleged "polemical relationship between the two plays," focusing on Good Deeds as well as Confession, in his essay on "*Everyman* and the Reformation," *Parergon*, No. 29 (1981), 24-31.

693. *God*: M *godts* (variant not listed in Vos).

707. *Met vijf woerden*: *Hoc est enim Corpus Meum* (For this is My body). Cf. Matthew 26.26.

730-33. On the keeping of concubines by priests in the Low Countries, Cooper and Wortham cite a sermon delivered by Gerard Groote in the cathedral of Utrecht in 1383 and known as *Contra focaristas* (*The Summoning of Everyman*, p. 48, note to 761-62).

749. *roeyken*: a notable crux. *Roeyken* is not documented in the *Mnl. W.* in the sense of *cross*, but according to a stage direction in *Homulus*, the Latin translation of *Elck.*, Confession supplies a cross to Elckerlijc. Editors tend to hesitate between *cross* and *pilgrim's staff* (cf. Van Elslander); Vos combines both interpretations: "probably a little cross that Elckerlijc as pilgrim carries with him."

756. *hebben*: B, H, M; L lacking.

760. *Sterck*: M; B, H *Sterc*; L *Streck*.

762. *beven*: M; L, B, H *boven*. Presumably *boven*, strange in this context, is a printing error (*bovengaen* = *win* or *gain the upper hand*; cf. *Mnl. W.*, I, 1409, under *bovengaen*). Endepols accepts the emendation *bogen* (*to bend, bow*), which, as Van Mierlo notes (p. 88), is influenced by the translation "folde" in *Everyman*: "My lymmes under me do folde."

767. *deser*: B, H, M; L *desen*.

786. *Ende*: H; L, B *En*; M *Ay*.

801. *ter kore*: Vos seems to suggest that *kore* is related to *chorus* or *choir*, but *coor* is masculine or neuter (*Mnl. W.*, III, 1855, under *coor*), whereas "ter" implies a feminine gender; see ibid., 1895, under *core* (*choice*).

815. *lenen*: editorial (B, H, L, *leven*; M *Leven*).

828. *allene*: B (M *alleene*); H, L *alleen*.

837. *Neemter*: B, H; M *neempt hier*; L *Neemt*.

838. The beginning of a rondel.

841. *Doch*: B, H, M; L *Duecht*. "Doch" parallels the conjunction "Ende" (838) and "Nu" (844); in 839 and 845 "Duecht" is referred to in the third person; from 838 and 844 it is obvious that "merct" is an imperative. Therefore "Doch" is the original.

872. *ter*: B, H, M; L lacking.

881. *voer*: B, H, M; L *van*.

882. *gadi*: glossed by Vos as "vergaat ge" ("you will perish"), but the *Mnl. W.* does not mention this meaning, and if indeed it can be documented, it must be very rare.

884. *talen*: B, M; H, L *tale*.

NOTES ON THE TEXT OF *EVERYMAN*

The four early prints of *Everyman* are designated, for the convenience of the reader, as in Cawley: the Huntington Library copy, the base text, as A; the Huth copy in the British Library as B; the Douce fragment in the Bodleian Library as C; the British Library fragment as D.

Editorial expansions are bracketed.

28. *rod*: B; A *rood*.

29. The unwarranted emendation of "lawe" to *love* persists (cf. David Bevington, ed., *Medieval Drama* [Boston, 1975], p. 941). Both the translator and Henri Logeman in his parallel-text edition of *Elckerlijc* and *Everyman* contributed to this crux (see *Notes and Queries*, N.S., 27 [1980], 298-99).

31. *theves*: B; A lacking.

111. *ado*: B; A *I do*.

156. *acqeintaunce*: editorial (A *acqueynce*, B *aqueyntaunce*).

251. *maketh*: B; A *make*.

271. *said*: B (*sayd*): A *say*.

286. *remembre*: B; A *remenbre*.

301. *endinge*: editorial (A, B *ende*).

303. *thus*: B; A *this*.

317. Ellipsis: A, B, D *go*.

324. *we*: B, D; A lacking.

325. *holde*: B, D; A *bolde*.

326. *bolde*: B, D; A *holde*.

417. *sholdest*: editorial (B, D *shuldest*; A *sholdes*).

453. *caught*; B, D; A *caugh*.

471. *forsoke*: D; A B *forsake*.

526. *be*: B, D; A *by*.

526. *creature*: also B, D. Despite W.W. Greg (cf. Cooper and Wortham, p. 34), the emendation *creater*, though it removes the faulty rime, is to be resisted since *creature* was a not uncommon spelling variant (see Cawley's note, p. 33, and the *M.E.D.* under *creatour*, 1 a, b).

527. *she*: editorial (A, B, D *he*).

549. *Repent*: D; A *Redempte*; B *Redempe*. Though "Redempte" is regularly accepted (cf. Cawley's text), to have Everyman declare himself saved at this point is illogical and presumptuous; moreover, as W.W. Greg shows, this reading is not supported by *Elckerlijc*, 514 (*Everyman* in *Materialien zur Kunde des älteren Englischen Dramas*, ed. W. Bang [Louvain, 1910], XXVIII, 64-65). On *repent* in the sense of *repentant*, see *O. E. D.* under *repent* a².

558. Ellipsis: editorial (A *voyce*; B, D lacking).

572. *The oile of forgivenes*: Cawley, followed by Cooper and Wortham, as well as by Trapp (*Oxford Anthology of English Literature*, I), identifies this phrase, which was thrown in by the translator, with Extreme Unction, but such an identification is far-fetched (see John Conley, "The Phrase 'The Oyle of Forgyuenes' in *Everyman*," *Notes and Queries*, N. S., 22 [1975], 105-06).

587. *me*: B, D; A lacking.

653. *it*: B; *them* D; A lacking.

660. *Dyscrecyon*: that is, Prudence, not "the faculty of discrimination, the power to make judgment on sensory perception" (Cooper and Wortham, *The Summoning of Everyman*, p. 42). Cf. John Conley, "The Identity of Discretion in *Everyman*," *Notes and Queries*, N.S., 30 (1983), 394-96.

671. *wolde*: B, D; A *wyll*.

678. *may*: B, D; A *myght*.

720. *pine*: B (*pyne*); A, C, D *payne*.

727. *devinite*: C, D (*deuynyte, deuinyte*); B *dyuynyte*; A *deuyuyte*.

739. *handes*: B, D; A *hande*.

753. *seven sacramentes*: editorial (A, B, C, D *same sacrament*); see *Elck.*, 723-24.

778. *rodde*: also B, C, D. Presumably a spelling error for *rood* (*cross*); see Cawley's note, pp. 36-37.

780. *our*: B, C, D; A *your*.

786. *Strength* (speaker): D; A, B, C *Knowlege*.

787. This imposing reference to one of the Nine Worthies is the translator's addition. The reference is ironical; long before the appearance of *Everyman*, the Nine Worthies had come to exemplify a commonplace central to the play, the vanity of the world (see *Notes and Queries*, N. S., 14 [1967], 50-51).

789. *do*: B, C, D; A *doth*.

804. *wolde*: B, D; A *woldest*.

868. *loved*: B, C, D; A *love*.

897. *thy. . .thy*: B, D; A *the. . .the*.

908. *for*: B, C, D; A lacking.

Costerus

Volume 13.
VINCENT DIMARCO and LESLIE PERELMAN: The Middle English Letter of Alexander to Aristotle. Amsterdam 1978. 194 p.   Hfl. 40,—

Volume 14.
JOHN W. CRAWFORD: Discourse: Essays on English and American Literature. Amsterdam 1978. 200 p.   Hfl. 40,—

Volume 15.
ROBERT F. WILLSON, Jr.: Landmarks of Shakespeare Criticism. Amsterdam 1978. 113 p.   Hfl. 25,—

Volume 16.
A.H. QURESHI: Edinburgh Review and Poetic Truth. Amsterdam 1978. 61 p.   Hfl. 15,—

Volume 17.
RAYMOND J.S. GRANT: Cambridge Corpus Christi College 41: The Loricas and the Missal. Amsterdam 1978. 127 p.   Hfl. 30,—

Volume 18.
CARLEE LIPPMAN: Lyrical Positivism. Amsterdam 1978. 195 p. Hfl. 40,—

Volume 19.
EVELYN A. HOVANEC: Henry James and Germany. Amsterdam 1978. 149 p.   Hfl. 30,—

Volume 20.
SANDY COHEN: Norman Mailer's Novels. Amsterdam 1979. 133 p.   Hfl. 25,—

Volume 21.
HANS BERTENS: The Fiction of Paul Bowles. The Soul is the Weariest Part of the Body. Amsterdam 1979. 260 p.   Hfl. 50,—

Volume 22.
RICHARD MANLEY BLAU: The Body Impolitic. A Reading of Four Novels by Herman Melville. Amsterdam 1979. 214 p.   Hfl. 45,—

Volume 23.
FROM CAXTON TO BECKETT: Essays presented by W.H. Toppen on the Occasion of his Seventieth Birthday, Edited by Jacques B.H. Alblas and Richard Todd. With a foreword by A.J. Fry. Amsterdam 1979. 133 p.   Hfl. 30,—

Volume 24.
CAROL JOHNSON: The Disappearance of Literature. Amsterdam 1980. 123 p.   Hfl. 25,—

Volume 25.
LINGUISTIC STUDIES offered to Berthe Siertsema, edited by D.J. van Alkemade, A. Feitsma, W.J. Meys, P. van Reenen en J.J. Spa. Amsterdam 1980. 382 p.   Hfl. 56,—

Volume 46.

STUDIES IN SEVENTEENTH-CENTURY ENGLISH LITERATURE, HISTORY AND BIBLIOGRAPHY. Festschrift for Professor T.A. Birrell on the occasion of his Sixtieth Birthday. Edited by G.A.M. Janssens and F.G.A.M. Aarts. Amsterdam 1984. 274 pp.   Hfl. 60,—

Contents: Preface. A.F. Allison: The "Mysticism" of Manchester Al Mondo. Some Catholic borrowings in a seventeenth-century Anglican work of devotion. A.G.H. Bachrach: General Othello's Service. F.J.M. Blom: Lucas Holstenius (1596-1661) and England. J.M. Blom: A German Jesuit and his Anglican Readers: The case of Jeremias Drexelius (1581-1638). Hans Bots: Jean Leclerc as Journalist of the Bibliothèques. His contribution to the spread of English learning on the European continent. D.E.L. Crane: Richard Stanyhurst's Translation of Vergil's Aeneid (1582). A.I. Doyle: The Library of Sir Thomas Tempest: Its origins and dispersal. Mirjam M. Foot: Some Bindings for Charles I. Johan Gerritsen: A Jonson Proof-Sheet — Neptunes Triumph. Wytze and Lotte Hellinga: Between Two Languages: Caxton's translation of Reynaert de Vos. F.J.M. Korsten: Thomas Baker's Reflections upon Learning. Hans Pörnbacher: English Virtue in Bavarian Baroque Literature: Mary Ward and her biographer Marcus Fridl. J.G. Riewald: The English Actors in the Low Countries, 1585 - c. 1650: An annotated bibliography. David Rogers: Antony Batt: A forgotten Benedictine translator. Irène Simon: Stillingfleet's Sermon Preached Before the King on the Anniversary of the Execution of Charles I (30 January 1668/9). Anna E.C. Simoni: John Wodroephe's Spared Houres. D.R.M. Wilkinson: Sospetto d'Herode: A neglected Crashaw poem. J. Anthony Williams: No-Popery Violence in 1688: Revolt in the provinces. A Checklist of the Writings of T.A. Birrell.

Volume 47.

FREDERIC WILL: Shamans in Turtlenecks: Selected Critical Essays 1958-1982. Amsterdam 1984. 304 pp.   Hfl. 60,—

Literature, an reflection onto it, are the theme. Few of these essays, however, deal with specific texts or the world-material those texts digest. The chief stress is on the nature of literature, of thought about literature, and of translation — the conversion of one text into its different twin in another language. The first section addresses the way literature knows and the ways we know literature. (The example-zone tends to be Greek, but the issues are general). The problematic leans toward a single knot: is sense-knowledge possible? What can the senses find out for themselves, as they are deployed in literature? Then, with essays on Solon and Prometheus, attention shifts to the creator's self-awareness. Literature as self-conscious sense knowledge comes into focus. The argument moves to translation, and the stress again falls on problematic knot: is translation possible, and under what conditions? The third zone — criticism and critique — looks at the individual's reconstruction of literary culture. Stress falls on subjectivity, which is the necessary condition for revivifying the other, the cultural object of knowledge. One particular example comes forth: the reconstruction of Herondas' work from the debris of fragments. Finally — the last two sections — a number of essays on the genesis, inner construction, and ultimate ambitions of the literary text. The sections open with a discussion of the heroic in literature, and conclude with the gods, ultimate fiction-denizens. Sandwiched between these flights, a group of essays on the mind-depths, the psychic well, from which the postulating word surges; as well as on the nature of the characters created from such depths. The source of texts — in naming — teases the argument into a final clarity.

Volume 48.

PAGE TO STAGE. *Theatre as Translation.* Edited by Ortrun Zuber-Skerritt. Amsterdam 1984. 200 pp.   Hfl. 45,—

Page to Stage deals with various aspects of transposing the dramatic script on to the stage or, vice versa, the creation of drama through processes of theatre productions. The authors are dramatists, theatre directors/producers, critics, actors, and teachers of drama from America, Europe, China, and mainly Australia. The book discusses practical problems of transposition, that is, 'translations' on stage, theatre performances, and production processes, processes of transposing or transferring the dramatic (original or translated) text on to the stage. This dramatic transposition is a specialized form of translation unique to drama and different from translating poetry or narrative prose. A play written for a performance must be actable and speakable. Therefore, non-verbal and cultural aspects as well as staging problems have to be taken into consideration. Each chapter is proceded by a short abstract to introduce the reader to the author's approach and main arguments. The book is aimed at readers interested in theatre generally, at active theatre groups, and at students and teachers of drama and of translation science.

IN PREPARATION

LITERATURE AND LORE OF THE SEA. Edited by Patricia Ann Carlson.
Contents: Emilio DeGrazia, Amber Waves of Grain: Rolvagg's Prairie Sea as Midwestern Metaphor and Myth. Haskell Springer, The American Sea Narrative: Fact and Form. Nancy W. Hutson, The Baptismal Fount: A Study of Sea Imagery in Kate Chopin's *The Awakening*. Dennis Berthold, Cape Horn Passages: Literary Conventions and Nautical Realities. Robert Foulke, Captain Alistown's Choice: The Ambiguities of Command at Sea. Glenn S. Burne, Captain Frederick Marryat: Romancer and Moralist. James M. Hughes, Dana, Cooper, Dickinson, and Roberts: Inner and Outer Seas. Ailene S. Goodman, Death and the Mermaid in Baroque Literature. Allan A. Arnold, The Equator-Crossing Ceremony — Origins and Purposes. Richard L. Wixon, Herman Melville: Critic of America and Harbinger of Ecological Crisis. Ronald DiLorenze, Jaws, or, the Mastication of Some Popular Sea Formulas. Edward L. Richards Jr., John Sherburne Sleeper (1794-1878) as Nautical Writer. Dennis Berthold, Joshua Slocum and the New England Literary Tradition; or, How Seaworthy Was Transcendentalism? Patricia Ann Carlson, Nathaniel Hawthorne and the Sea. John Z. Guzlowski, No More Sea Changes: Four Recent American Novelists' Responses to the Sea. Walter L. Barker, Patterns and Images in the Naming of Sea Craft. Emilio DeGrazia, Poe's Other Beautiful Woman. James M. Hughes, Popular Imagery of the Sea: Metaphor, Simile, Lore. Robert Gregory, The Reader at See in Hawkes' *Second Skin*. Jay S. Hoar, Real Life Ancient Mariners Among the Last of the Blue and the Gray. Kieran Quinlan, Sea and Sea-Shore as Image, Metaphore, and Rhythmic Influence in 'Song of Myself'. John L. Cobbs: Sea Change: Main Currents in Popular Sea Songs, 1956-1966. Bradley F. Millard, Searching for the Commercial Fisherman in Fiction and Fact: Steps Toward a Collection and a Bibliography. Robert D. Madison, Sea Songs and Chanteys of the Nineteenth Century. Normam Bagnall, The Selchie in Legend and Literature. Peggy Creighton, Social Behavior of Seamen. Ellen J. O'Brien, 'That Insular Tahiti': Melville's Truth-Seeker and the Sea.